AUTHOR	CLASS
WYLLIE, I.	598.74

TITLE	No.
Cuckoo	441787703

The Cuckoo

The Cuckoo

Ian Wyllie

B. T. Batsford Ltd. London

For Thomas and Jonathan

© Ian Wyllie 1981
First published 1981

ISBN 0 7134 0266 0

Typeset in Linotron Meridien, 10 on 12pt by
Western Printing Services Ltd, Bristol
and printed in Great Britain by
The Anchor Press Ltd, Tiptree, Essex

for the publishers B. T. Batsford Ltd
4 Fitzhardinge Street, London W1H 0AH

Contents

Acknowledgment

It was through wildlife film-maker Maurice Tibbles that my interest in cuckoos was first stimulated during the making of his film, *The Private Life of the Cuckoo* which won an award from the British Association for Science in 1976. We knew from the outset that to film a Cuckoo in the act of egg-laying was going to be the most difficult part, but it was, perhaps, because of that difficulty, and the great sense of achievement when it had been 'canned', that our enthusiasm was kept alive. Anyone who has worked with, or knows, Maurice, will appreciate his artistic and technical skill at filming wildlife, and to combine that with a dedication and zest for success cannot fail to give inspiration, as it did me, to those around him or those who see his films.

I am indebted also to the many landowners and farmers around St Ives, Fen Drayton, Swavesey, Over and Woodwalton in Cambridgeshire, to the Nature Conservancy Council responsible for Monks Wood and Woodwalton Fen National Nature Reserves, and to British Rail (Eastern) and Amalgamated Roadstone Company (Eastern Region), for allowing me unrestricted access to their respective land.

I owe my gratitude to many friends and colleagues at Monks Wood Experimental Station who have helped in a multitude of ways during my study of Cuckoos from caterpillar-identification by Nick Greatorix-Davies to the many useful discussions about cuckoo problems with John Parslow, Dan Osborne, Robert Kenwood, and Peter Ward. I owe a special debt of thanks to Dr Ian Newton who has commented on and criticized most of this book in earlier drafts. His advice and encouragement have been of enormous help.

This book owes much to the writings of many research workers on other cuckoos who are acknowledged in the text or bibliography. In particular, the books by Edgar Chance and E. C. Stuart Baker, written nearly 40 years ago, I found stimulating reading. My ideas and writing have been much influenced by the works of H. Friedmann who has made a life-long and monumental contribution to our knowledge of brood parasites, of R. B. Payne and A. F. Skutch and of David Lack.

Finally, I am indebted to my wife who, during the last eight years, has endured long periods of neglect, disturbed sleep as I crept out before daybreak to catch cuckoos, and who has contended with constant 'cuckoo-talk' to the exclusion of all other conversation. I thank her for the many valuable discussions and for her unfailing encouragement and support, without which this book may never have been written.

List of Illustrations

Black and white photographs
Between pages 32 and 33
1 Maurice Tibbles setting up his camera before entering a hide
2 The author about to enter a hide
3 Part of the study site at St Ives, Cambridgeshire
4 Wing-tagged young Cuckoo (75N)
5 Male Cuckoo
6 Cuckoo and Sparrowhawk
7 Female Reed Warbler brooding her clutch
8 Female Cuckoo watching a reedbed
9 and 10 Female Cuckoo robbing the eggs of a nest she does not intend to parasitize
11 Female Cuckoo robbing a nest
12 Female Cuckoo robbing a Reed Warbler's nest
13 Willow Warbler attacking the head of a Cuckoo

Between pages 64 and 65
14 Reed Warbler feeding a 12-day old Cuckoo
15 Caterpillars of the buff-tip moth
16 Caterpillar of the gold-tail moth
17 and 18 Two common hosts of the Cuckoo: Redstarts and Dunnock
19 and 20 Female Cuckoo approaching a Reed Warbler's nest
21 Female Cuckoo holding one of the warbler's eggs in her bill
22 Cuckoo's egg in a Reed Warbler's clutch
23 Young Cuckoo shortly after hatching
24 and 25 Young Cuckoo ejecting the eggs of the Reed Warbler

Between pages 96 and 97
26 Young Cuckoo, two days old
27 Young Cuckoo, four days old
28 Young Cuckoo, six days old
29 Young Cuckoo, 12 days old

Colour plates

Introduction

Perhaps no other bird has aroused quite as much interest and speculation in the minds of Man as the subject of this book, the Common or
European Cuckoo, *Cuculus canorus*. It is a bird that has been written
about since biblical times when Moses branded the 'Cuckow' along with
vultures and birds of prey as a creature to be 'held in abomination'.
Obviously its unorthodox habits were common knowledge then, as
they certainly were to Aristotle in about 300 BC. For over 2,000 years
now the Cuckoo has been a subject of great mystery and conjecture,
reaching an almost legendary status rare for a living bird. It has featured
extensively in European folklore through the ages – and great artists,
whether they be poets, playwrights or musical composers, have not
failed to include the Cuckoo in their works. In the last 60 years or so,
much has been learnt of its general habits and behaviour, but we are still
largely ignorant of the means by which the Cuckoo's unconventional
lifestyle has evolved.

The European Cuckoo is one of several closely related species, which
are renowned for not building nests of their own; laying their eggs in
the nests of foster species (hosts) which incubate the eggs and rear the
young. The hosts do this nearly always to the detriment of their own
brood. The cuckoos are not alone in adopting such a reproductive
strategy (known technically as *obligate brood parasitism*) for it occurs in
five different bird families. These include the *Molothrus* cowbirds
(Icteridae) of the Americas, the honeyguides (Indicatoridae) of Africa
and Asia, the widowbirds and the Cuckoo-weaver, *Anomalospiza imoerbis*
(Ploceidae) of Africa, the Black-headed Duck, *Heteronetta atricapilla* (Ana-
tidae) of tropical South America, and two subfamilies of cuckoos (Cuculinae with 47 species and Neomorphinae with three parasitic species,
together comprising the family Cuculidae). The duck is the odd one out
because, while all the others require parental care of their young from
their respective hosts, the Black-headed Duck demands only that its
eggs are incubated. Soon after they hatch the ducklings become entirely
independent of all parental care and fend for themselves. Even

ducklings reared in captivity dissociated themselves from their foster
parent and attempted to escape (Weller 1968).

The parasitic lifestyle is evidently quite rare in the animal kingdom as
a whole. Among other vertebrates, only a few species of fish are known
to be parasitic in the same way as brood parasitic birds. Among the lower
animals, some insects, notably the cuckoo-bee (*Psithryus*) and the
cuckoo-wasp, *Vespa austriaca*, lay their eggs into the nests of other
insects which then rear the parasites. Otherwise no other animal requir-
ing parental care for its offspring is known regularly to parasitize other
animals.

In all there are about 80 known species of brood parasitic birds
although this number is likely to increase as more birds are studied. At
the moment they represent only about 1 per cent of the world's bird
species. Such a low incidence illustrates perhaps that brood parasitism is
no easy course to follow, but it does not mean that it is unprofitable for
the successful practitioners. The Common Cuckoo is perhaps not a
locally abundant species, but it is extremely widespread. In its breeding
range alone it extends from Ireland in the west, across Eurasia to Japan
and from the tundra in the north to the deserts of the Middle East and
North Africa (Figure 1). In this range it spends only 2–4 months of the
year. At other times, it occurs throughout the tropics of Africa and
south-east Asia as far south as the southern coast of South Africa. To
avoid cumbersome use of references in the text only the most pertinent
sources are given; a full bibliography is given on pages 160–169.

Evolution of brood parasitism

The fundamental question of how brood parasitism evolved remains
unsolved, but there is no shortage of theories on the subject. Baker
(1942), for example, proposed that parasitic cuckoos evolved directly
from reptiles so that they never developed a nest-building ability in the
first place, but this ignores the phyletic position of cuckoos within the
bird class. On the contrary, they almost certainly evolved from non-
parasitic bird ancestors; so long ago that the reasons for becoming
parasitic are now obscure.

In *The Origin of Species*, Darwin suggested that the occasional or perhaps accidental laying of eggs by one species into the nest of another
initiated the development of brood parasitism. He instanced the case of
the North American non-parasitic *Coccyzus* cuckoos which lay eggs
normally in nests of their own but sometimes in nests of other unrelated species; he believed that if such occasional behaviour was beneficial to the adults or young then, by inheritance and natural selection,

the habit would become enhanced and rapidly spread through the population to produce the kind of cuckoos we have today. In most cases, however, eggs so disposed would not survive. They might be the wrong size for the host to incubate, or make the nest more conspicuous to predators, or be laid at the wrong time in relation to the host's incubation programme. The primitive parasitic cuckoo would not 'know' which hosts would accept and incubate its eggs, and rear its young, or at what time to introduce its egg into the nest to achieve success. These refinements would come through natural selection, only those cuckoos with appropriate behaviour perpetuating themselves by leaving offspring, and others with inappropriate behaviour dying out. Free from parental responsibilities, the cuckoo could also spend more time feeding and produce more eggs to offset the losses through rejection or failure by unsuitable host species.

Brood parasitism has sometimes been explained in terms of a breakdown or 'degeneration' of normal reproductive activities such as loss of nest-building or egg-laying and incubation patterns with associated endocrine imbalances. The non-parasitic cuckoos (subfamily Phaenicophinae) are well-known for building rather flimsy nests in which the eggs look precarious. This apparent poor nest-building ability, however, is not confined purely to non-parasitic cuckoos: doves and pigeons (Columbiformes), for example, build equally fragile nests and many other birds (e.g. some falcons) never build their own, but occupy disused nests of other species in which they successfully rear their own young. So a loss of nest-building ability is not necessarily accompanied by a lack of parental care.

Wrongly-timed nest-building and egg-laying, with eggs ready for laying prior to nest construction, has also been suggested as initiating brood parasitism. Many birds may suffer nest loss before they have laid the first egg, so any bird in fact may occasionally have an egg ready to be laid, but no nest of its own ready to receive it. Normally in such cases the formed egg is laid on the ground and wasted, the developing ova are resorbed, and another nest is built in time for a new clutch within a relatively short period. If an individual bird enjoyed only occasional success by laying an egg in the nest of another species, this does not mean that the entire species would become parasitic. Something much more fundamental would be required to alter the breeding habits of the entire population.

For the cowbirds, a group which contains both nesting and parasitic species, Friedmann (1929) proposed a phylogenetic model in which the various degrees of parasitism represented evolutionary stages of development. He proposed a progressive reduction of male territorial behaviour from the primitive to the climax species; contributing in turn to reduced breeding success and the development of the parasitic mode of reproduction. The cowbirds consist of the Bay-winged Cowbird, *Molothrus badius*, which may steal the nest of another species but rears its own young. *M. badius* is the exclusive host of the Screaming Cowbird, *M. rufoaxillaris*. The Giant Cowbird, *Scaphidura orizivora*, parasitizes other Icteridae as does the Bronzed Cowbird, *M. aeneus*, the latter also victimizing Fringillidae hosts. The Shiny Cowbird, *M. bonariensis*, parasitizes a variety of small passerine hosts but does not seem to have evolved any egg-mimicry with different species. Finally the Brown-headed Cowbird, *M. ater*, of North America parasitizes a great variety of passerine hosts with a few of which it has evolved accurate egg-mimicry.

More recently, Payne (1977) has suggested that brood parasitism may be 'an evolutionary strategy to spread the risks of predation'. By dispersing eggs in many nests an individual brood parasite increases its chances of leaving more offspring. Payne calculated that the increased chance of survival of at least one egg with scatter-laying is 20 per cent where the host has a high nest survival, but where the host has low nest survival the increased chance of success is more than double that when all the eggs are laid in one nest. Certainly most brood parasites lay their eggs singly into several nests but some do not, and there is no reason to suppose that the latter are any less successful or more highly evolved than the majority. If dispersed laying evolved in birds to reduce predation and increase chances of survival, it is difficult to see why this method of reproduction did not develop in more groups than the five families (or parts of families) of brood parasites existing today.

One final hypothesis for the evolution of brood parasitism, as proposed by Hamilton and Orians (1965) and agreed by Lack (1968), is especially applicable to the cuckoos and honeyguides. Both these groups have specialized diets which might be thought unsuitable for rearing their own young. Adult honeyguides eat wax produced by social insects. In a recent study in Nepal of the Orange-rumped Honeyguide, *Indicator xanthonotus*, Cronin and Sherman (1977) found that a male established a 'territory' by a bee's nest which was defended against rival males but advertised to attract many females. The male mated with each female and allowed them access to the food. Unfortunately these workers could not prove that this species in Asia was parasitic like its African relatives. African honeyguides are known to have special bacteria in their digestive systems which digest wax, but they also eat insects at times. Cuckoos specialize on hairy and toxic caterpillars which might be thought unsuitable food items for their young. However, this diet is not confined to just the parasitic species: non-parasitic cuckoos rear their young on apparently similar food. It is possible, nevertheless, that nesting cuckoo species bring other foods to their young (e.g. grasshoppers) and, until a more detailed dietary comparison between the two groups has been made, it is pointless to elaborate on this hypothesis. Nolan and Thompson (1975) found that during years of superabundant food (i.e. when there were outbreaks of certain periodic insects) in North America, *Coccyzus* non-parasitic cuckoos laid larger clutches in their own nests as well as laying in other nests of their own kind, or in nests of totally unrelated birds. These cuckoos therefore became parasitic when they could gather more food than was necessary to rear their normal broods.

A relationship between periodic food supply and brood parasitism can be envisaged for the other groups. The cowbirds find food partly by following large herd animals, so prior to the introduction of domestic cattle, they might have kept on the move with the foraging animals. This would have reduced their breeding time in any one area, while brood parasitism would allow successful reproduction without the burden of territorial maintenance and parental care.

Similarly, in the tropics many birds have their breeding season synchronized with a short period of abundant food supply following very seasonal rains. A bird which specialized on a particular diet within such a short period might experience a period of good food supply too short for it to produce a nest, lay eggs, and rear young to independence.

It is also possible that brood parasitism evolved by different routes in the various groups. This is perhaps more especially true for the parasitic duck which is the only precocial species and is the least damaging to its hosts. There are also several species of ducks, geese and gamebirds which not uncommonly lay eggs into the nests of neighbouring species, while they rear a brood of their own. Whether such behaviour would lead to complete parasitism in a species, as has been suggested, is debatable.

Whatever the evolutionary history of brood parasitism may be, there is no doubt that this method of reproduction is highly adapted and the subject of this book, the European Cuckoo, shows some of the most advanced adaptations known in broodparasitic birds. In the following chapters I have attempted to present the known facts and current theories on the ecology and general biology of this poorly studied but world famous bird. In particular there are data from a six-year field study of Cuckoos parasitizing Reed Warblers, *Acrocephalus scirpaceus*, at one main and several subsidiary sites in Cambridgeshire, England.

The background to research in Cambridgeshire

This study began in 1973 with the making of a wildlife film on Cuckoos under the direction of Maurice Tibbles. Conveniently close to my home, we discovered that 12 out of 15 Reed Warbler nests had been parasitized. Here was an ideal site of riverside and gravel pit reedbeds where there was a plentiful supply of both Cuckoos and Reed Warblers, the latter nesting in predictable and accessible sites which facilitated nest-finding. After an exhaustive examination of Cuckoos in other British habitats using different host species, Tibbles decided that this Cambridgeshire site provided the best opportunity for the completion of his film, which was hopefully to include sequences of the egg-laying by a female Cuckoo. Without prior knowledge, the task of even seeing a laying seemed almost impossible. How could one predict where and when a particular Cuckoo would lay one of its eggs? Yet 50 years ago, a record of egg-laying had been obtained using black and white film in a hand-cranked camera, and the answer lay in two books written by Edgar Chance: *The Cuckoo's Secret* (1922) and *The Truth About the Cuckoo* (1940). Chance was an egg-collector who made a detailed study of Cuckoos parasitizing an isolated group of Meadow Pipits, *Anthus pratensis*, on a small common in Worcestershire. By concentrating on one female (Cuckoo A) he soon confirmed earlier reports by Baldamus (1892) and Rey (1892) that a particular female Cuckoo parasitized only one main host species and that its eggs tended to be laid at two-day intervals, in the afternoons, and directly into nests containing incomplete host clutches. Chance found that he could identify a female by its unique egg-colour and pattern, and by manipulating the nesting of the pipits through destroying their nests and eggs, he induced Cuckoo A to lay 25 eggs in a single season. He accurately predicted where she would lay on a given occasion by knowing her laying pattern and the location and stage of development of all the available host nests. Thus he was able to show many people a Cuckoo laying and was able to obtain film and photographs on numerous occasions.

Using Chance's findings from the 1920s, Maurice Tibbles and I were successful in 1974 in filming once again, and, as far as we knew, in colour for the first time, Cuckoos in the act of laying their eggs, but this time into Reed Warbler nests. The resulting film, *The Private Life of the Cuckoo*, produced by Jeffery Boswell of the BBC Natural History Unit at Bristol, was first shown on British television in July 1975. Unknown to us at the time, Messrs E. and T. Channel of Southampton were also making a television film called *The Petersfinger Cuckoos* featuring Cuckoos and Reed Warblers around the village of Petersfinger in Hampshire. These films give detailed and accurate accounts of breeding British Cuckoos and both received a world circulation.

Our present understanding of the Cuckoo's mode of reproduction is broadly as follows: it has been reasonably established that individual females tend to parasitize only one main host species and lay many eggs singly into different nests at two-day intervals during the host's laying period. They are inclined to lay all their eggs in a more or less restricted area, tending towards individual egg-laying territories. Without individually marking them, each female can only be identified with certainty by its unique egg-type which remains the same throughout its life, irrespective of the male. The evidence for this rests on the work of those egg-collectors in the past throughout Europe who attempted to find all the eggs laid in particular areas. By finding the eggs as they were laid at two-day intervals it has been shown that each female's eggs remain the same in colour and pattern during the season and from year to year. Mimetic resemblance of Cuckoo eggs to the eggs of different host species has led to the development of the 'gens' concept in which each Cuckoo allegedly belongs to a separate genetic strain or 'clan' according to its choice of host and associated egg-mimicry. Thus there are special Reed Warbler-Cuckoos, Pied Wagtail-Cuckoos, pipit-Cuckoos and so on. In any one region it is rare to find more than two or three gens living together, and several which occur commonly on the European continent do not appear in Britain. Male Cuckoos are believed to establish territories from which they exclude rival males and attract mates by their loud, characteristic songs uttered from exposed vantage points. Young birds are thought to parasitize later the same host species which reared them, either through genetic inheritance of host-specificity or through a form of 'host-imprinting' originating in the host nest, or even through 'habitat-imprinting'. Thus if a young Cuckoo learned to recognize either its host or its host's habitat, it could return and select the appropriate host for its eggs in later life.

From Chance's findings in the 1920s, others' since, and our own field experiences during the making of *The Private Life of the Cuckoo*, it became clear that many of these ideas on the Cuckoo's adaptations to suit brood parasitism as well as the evolutionary and hereditary implications of those adaptations were still only at the theory stage, although they are widely accepted in the ornithological literature. It has never actually been shown, for example, that a young Cuckoo returns to parasitize the species that it was reared by. The difficulties of making field observations on such secretive, non-nesting and wide-ranging birds have probably hampered field research, so little progress has been made since Chance's day.

Nevertheless, the ornithological literature is rife with theories on various cuckoo problems, some plausible but unsubstantiated and others improbable or far-fetched. One example was the method of egg deposition by the female. It was formerly believed that the usual method was for the female to lay on the ground, then to carry the egg to an appropriate nest, even 'choosing' a nest in which the eggs resembled her own. This was based on the sighting of females carrying eggs in their beaks. Edgar Chance completely refuted this idea, at least for Cuckoos parasitizing Meadow Pipits, and he was able to show that the Cuckoo was in fact carrying away one of the host's eggs. So firm was the belief in the former method that many ornithologists did not believe Chance's evidence and perhaps there are sceptics even today.

A more recent example of unfounded conjecture was proposed by Ackworth (1955). To explain the presence of Cuckoo eggs in apparently inaccessible nests, this author suggested that Cuckoos were hybrids resulting from the mating of the male parasite with the female host. Such an idea is too ridiculous for comment, but it illustrates the degree to which imagination may stretch with an almost total disregard for biological facts.

Having accidentally discovered a suitable breeding site and learnt a certain amount about the Cuckoos parasitizing Reed Warblers during the making of our film in 1973–1974, it seemed to me well worth attempting to study these birds further. One of the main problems we had encountered was that we could not identify the individual birds that we saw; even the sex could not always be determined. There was also more than one male apparently using the same area, and from their different egg-types we found that six females were laying eggs in 1974. I resolved therefore in future years to catch and mark Cuckoos for individual recognition in the field. Coloured leg rings would be no use since they would be hidden by the feathered tarsi and in any case one rarely saw a bird close enough to see its legs. The only convenient solution at that time was to use coloured wing-tags which could be easily and inexpensively attached to the patagial membrane of the wings, and would allow identification of one bird over the whole season and hopefully in subsequent years. Knowing that Cuckoos respond to imitations of their songs and calls, particularly in the first few weeks after arrival, I proposed to catch them in mist nets using tape-recordings and a stuffed specimen. I was anxious not to disturb the breeding behaviour of the birds and limited my catching attempts to that period from arrival in late April until egg-laying began in late May, a period of only three or four weeks. I prepared myself in the early spring of 1975, and the first permanent singing male arrived at the breeding site on 24 April. The bird responded immediately to tape-recordings of male song and after a concerted effort, and to my great delight, it became caught in the net later that same day. The method worked; the wing-tag instantly identified the bird at great distance and did not appear adversely to affect its flight. Subsequent arriving Cuckoos, however, proved much more difficult or impossible to catch. There were few suitable places where mist nets could be erected and remain free from the risk of human interference. The birds could also see the nets in daylight, whereas they could not see them so well at dawn and dusk when, fortunately, Cuckoos appeared to be most active. Weather also affected my catching success: strong winds or heavy rain prevented any activities and further reduced the amount of time that could be spent on catching attempts. It soon became clear in 1975 that, despite the first-day success, it was not going to be possible to catch and mark all the birds using the site. I therefore had to concentrate where possible on the marked birds and try to fit unmarked ones into the picture. Between 1975 and 1979, a total of 22 adult and 60 nestling Cuckoos were tagged or ringed in Cambridgeshire. Of the adults with wing-tags, only two males and one female were known to return to the same site in a subsequent year; the female was marked in 1976 and was seen in May 1977, but was recovered dead later that month. Of the 60 nestlings, one young female and three young males were found to return to their birthplaces in one or more later years. One male was marked as a nestling in 1975 and returned to the same site in 1976, 1977 and 1978, but not in 1979. Another wing-tagged nestling was marked on 13 July 1978 and was recovered alive at a bird ringing station in northern Italy on 28 August, only six weeks later.

With these individually marked birds I was hoping to investigate a range of Cuckoo problems that could not be answered without knowing individuals in the field. For example, there had always been doubt about whether the female could produce the 'cuck-oo' call, and conversely on whether the male occasionally uses the female 'bubbling' call. Since the sex of an individual cannot always be determined in the field, this question could be answered using marked birds of known sex. It would also be possible to look at the social organization of Cuckoos: some people think they are monogamous, others regard them as polygynous (several females per male), polyandrous (several males per female) or promiscuous, but these ideas are all based on personal impressions with birds of unknown identity. With wing-tagged birds it would also be possible to investigate dispersion in both sexes in the field and whether or not they were territorial. Without this, the males are usually indistinguishable by appearance or song in the field, but the females can at least be identified by their eggs.

On a more long-term basis, by following the breeding activities of marked birds and of possible returning young Cuckoos of known parenthood, I particularly hoped to examine heredity of egg-type and of host-specificity. Would a young Cuckoo hatched from a particular egg-type and reared by Reed Warblers return to lay eggs of similar type and in nests of the same species? If enough young birds in their first breeding year could be located around the same site it would then be feasible to conduct an experiment in one year to remove all the Cuckoo eggs from Reed Warbler nests and relocate them into nests of another locally abundant species. The resulting young females would then have an egg-type suited to the original host species, and it would remain to be seen whether they subsequently parasitized the original host species or the foster species. If they parasitized their natural host, selection of host could be described as inherent, but if they parasitized the foster host, 'imprinting' would be implied. Some evidence of this kind is crucial to the whole concept of host-specific strains of European Cuckoos and their associated egg-mimicry. Sadly, as it has turned out, too few Cuckoos returned to the study site in subsequent years to make such an experiment worth conducting.

In conjunction with following the movements of Cuckoos from direct field observations, my main activity was the location and daily recording of all the nests of the Reed Warblers. The numbers of pairs occupying the region were probably consistent each year but because I intensively surveyed different areas each year, and because densities of the birds were very high in some reedbeds, the number of pairs could not be accurately estimated. The numbers of nests I found each year varied from 136 in 1974 to 324 in 1979, with an average of about 230 a year. Each pair of Reed Warblers produced more than one nest in a season; sometimes as many as six nests were made before a pair achieved success. A high rate of nest-loss necessitated frequent nest checks. If the nest failed at any stage for any reason, a new nest could be expected nearby within about a week. At my main study site near St Ives in Cambridgeshire, a total of 1,396 nests were found in 1974–1979; a further 368 were examined at other sites in Cambridgeshire, to give a total of 1,764 nests. Of this total, 1,367 nests produced eggs and were therefore suitable for Cuckoo parasitism, and in fact 170 were para-sitized by a total of 25 females in the six years. Six nests received two eggs, always of two different female Cuckoos. Two Sedge Warbler *Acrocephalus schoenobaenus* nests were also parasitized, but by female Cuckoos which normally laid their eggs in Reed Warbler nests. During the six-year study, therefore, I found 178 eggs or young of the Cuckoos.

Although several useful pieces of information have resulted from wing-tagging, in general I was hampered by too few observations of the birds, either because they were very secretive or too far-ranging. In addition, the tags may have come off, there may have been poor site-fidelity in the birds, and there may have been a high mortality, especially of my wing-tagged birds because of their increased conspicuousness. This last hazard was firmly brought home to me in 1979 when one of the tagged males was recovered dead and mostly eaten inside the nest of a Tawny Owl, *Strix aluco*, containing a large healthy youngster. On the whole, wing-tagging did not increase the number of observations of Cuckoos in the field and, since not all the birds could be caught, was of little use in assessing their social organization.

There is another tool that can be used by the field ecologist to follow the movements of individual animals closely. This is known as radio-telemetry, in which small radio transmitters are attached to an animal allowing an observer with a receiver to track one or several animals for as long as the batteries of the transmitters remain operative. The bigger the animal, the larger the battery that can be used and the larger the range and length of life of the transmitter. Cuckoos can carry a transmitter weighing about four or five grammes which may have a range of about three kilometres and a life of about eight weeks. Due to the efforts of my colleague, Dr Robert Kenward, I was able in 1979 to follow several Cuckoos during the breeding season with radio transmitters, and the exciting information that was gathered is reported in later chapters of this book.

1 | The Cuckoo Family

In Britain the Cuckoo tends to be regarded as a special bird in a class of its own. There are no other bird species which are parasitic, and few which have such a distinctive call. Most of the birds that are best known by their voices do not occur in such a wide variety of habitats throughout the land. But the Cuckoo is equally at home on a wild Scottish mountainside and in a sheltered lowland wood, and on a windswept treeless island or a reed-strewn dyke in the flat land of East Anglia.

While it may be unique in these respects in Britain and most of Europe, on a global scale the Cuckoo has no less than 49 parasitic and 77 non-parasitic relatives, which comprise the family Cuculidae. To put the European Cuckoo in its international context, this first chapter describes the classification, distributions and general characteristics of the world's cuckoos. Some of them have been extensively studied and documented; others are rare, poorly studied, and sometimes known only from a few tattered museum skins.

Members of the cuckoo family are found in all parts of the world, except for the polar regions where there is no food to support them. The majority of species breed in the tropics, especially in Africa and Asia. Those which breed elsewhere migrate to the tropics for their non-breeding season. The species have been classified into six subfamilies and 27 genera (Table 1).

The subfamilies

Parasitic cuckoos (Cuculinae)
The true parasitic cuckoos are distributed throughout the Old World. There are 12 genera with a total of 47 species, and 34 of these breed exclusively in the tropics of Africa, south-east Asia or Australasia.

Some or part of the populations of the other species migrate from the tropics to breed either in the Palaearctic or Australasian regions. The main migrants include five species in the genus *Cuculus*, all or some of which move north from the tropics to breed in Eurasia. The Great

Table 1 *The classification of the cuckoo family* Order: Cuculiformes Family: Cuculidae

Subfamily	Cuculinae (parasitic cuckoos)	Phaenicophaeinae (non-parasitic cuckoos)	Neomorphinae (ground cuckoos)	Crotophaginae (anis and guira)	Centropodinae (coucals)	Couinae (couas)
Genera (number of species)	*Cuculus* (12) *Clamator* (4) *Eudynamis* (2) *Cercococcyx* (3) *Chrysococcyx* (14) *Cacomantis* (6) *Pachycoccyx* (1) *Rhamphomantis* (1) *Caliechthrus* (1) *Surniculus* (1) *Microdynamis* (1) *Scythrops* (1)	*Phaenicophaeus* (12) *Coccyzus* (8) *Piaya* (5) *Saurothera* (2) *Ceuthmochares* (1)	*Neomorphus* (5) *Carpococcyx* (2) *Dromococcyx* (2) *Tapera* (1) *Morococcyx* (1)	*Crotophaga* (3) *Guira* (1)	*Centropus* (25)	*Coua* (10)

Figure 1. Breeding (shaded) and wintering (dashed) ranges of the Common Cuckoo, *Cuculus canorus*, and its subspecies

Spotted Cuckoo, *Clamator glandarius*, migrates north from tropical Africa to breed in southern Europe. Parasitic cuckoos which migrate south of the tropics to breed include the Long-tailed Koel, *Eudynamis taitensis*, which flies across miles of open sea from the South Pacific islands of Samoa, Tonga, and Fiji to New Zealand. Similarly, the New Zealand Shining Bronze Cuckoo, *Chrysococcyx lucidus*, is famed for its 3,000km migration entirely across ocean from the Solomon and Bismark Islands, a feat once thought remarkable for so small a bird (it measures about 16cm in length). Cuckoo migrations are highly seasonal, corresponding to the abundance of insects in the respective breeding and wintering ranges, and to the breeding seasons of the hosts. Even those cuckoo species which breed in the tropics migrate at times of food shortage and such movements are largely associated with the seasonal rains in these areas. No species of parasitic cuckoo is known to time its migration solely to coincide with its host's breeding season; many leave their breeding ranges when suitable hosts are still building nests and laying eggs.

Those species of Cuculinae which have been studied are all strictly brood parasitic, although with some variation. Neither the eggs or young of a dozen species have ever been discovered, so these birds are only suspected of being brood parasitic. They include three species of the genus *Cercococcyx* inhabiting dense tropical forests in Africa, seven species in New Guinea, one limited to the islands of the Moluccas, and a rare member of the genus *Chrysococcyx* of African forests (Table 2). Because of the remote parts of the world inhabited by these cuckoos, and the relatively inaccessible habitats occupied by them, they have eluded serious ornithological study.

Parasitic cuckoos are difficult birds to study anyway, because they are usually shy, unobtrusive (except for their voices), widely dispersed and rarely stay in one place for long. The 35 species which are known to be definitely parasitic include some which have been more extensively researched (e.g. Common Cuckoo), others which are generally known from several records, and still others which are known only from a few incidents of parasitism. Assumptions may have been made in the past for the poorly known species, based on our better knowledge of the others: these should be viewed with care until substantiated.

The 12 species in the genus *Cuculus* all parasitize small insectivorous birds such as pipits and wagtails (Motacillidae) or chats, babblers and Old World warblers (Muscicapidae). Each cuckoo species contains individuals which are host-specific, while the total range of host species of any one cuckoo may exceed 100. The eggs are small and polymorphic, with accurate mimicry of the eggs of some host species, poor of others. The young normally eject the young or unhatched eggs of the host from the nest, so that they are reared alone on all the food intended for the host's brood.

The small, brilliantly-coloured glossy or bronze cuckoos, *Chrysococcyx*, constitute another genus of 14 species found almost entirely in the tropics. Like the *Cuculus* group, these tiny cuckoos parasitize a great range of small host species and lay mimetic eggs singly into several nests. Their young are again raised to the exclusion of the host's brood, although a physical eviction instinct is not so pronounced. In some of the nests parasitized by these cuckoos it would seem impossible for the young cuckoo to eject the host's eggs or young, and in these cases it is suspected that the rapid growth of the young parasite enables it to outgrow and smother the host young. Probably the best known of them is the African Didric Cuckoo, *Chrysococcyx caprius*, which has been known to parasitize 67 different species, mainly weaverbirds (Friedmann 1968). Some of these hosts build defensive funnels on their nests through which it would seem impossible for a female Didric to gain access. How Didrics lay their eggs into such nests remains a mystery (but see Chapter 8).

Another group of small tropical parasitic cuckoos contains six species in the genus *Cacomantis* found between south-east Asia and Australia. These also parasitize small hosts and lay mimetic eggs. The Plaintive Cuckoo, *Cacomantis merulinus*, for example, parasitizes warblers (Sylviinae) some of which build domed nests with very small entrance holes. Baker (1942) described the remarkable degree of egg-mimicry between this cuckoo and its various host species. One common host in southern India is the Indian Wren-warbler, *Prinia inornata*, which lays a deep blue egg, blotched red or black. The eggs of the Plaintive Cuckoo laid in these nests are also blue and spotted with red. In a part of the Deccan the cuckoo parasitizes the Ashy Long-tailed Warbler, *Prinia socialis*, which lays a brilliant chestnut-red egg. The cuckoo faithfully mimics these by also laying red eggs. However, writes Baker, when the population of Ashy Long-tailed Warblers temporarily disappeared, the cuckoos attempted to parasitize the Indian Wren-warblers in the area. The result was that red cuckoo eggs were laid into nests containing blue host eggs, and the hosts deserted their nests.

At the other size extreme, the large Indian Koel, *Eudynamis scolopacea*, parasitizes the House Crow, *Corvus splendens*, and the young Koels are raised with the young crows. The male Koel lures the adult crows away from their nest while the female slips in, destroys a crow's egg and lays a mimetic egg in its place. One advantage of not ejecting nest-mates is that the female Koel can lay more than one egg in each nest with a good chance of having them accepted. As many as 16 eggs have been found in one crow's nest, but these may have been laid by several females. A problem with multiple laying and host-egg destruction is that the female Koel now has to distinguish between her previous eggs and those of the host, or risk destroying her own eggs.

Some parasitic cuckoos in the *Clamator* genus also sometimes lay more than one egg into the nests of their hosts and the young are again raised with the host young. These large crested cuckoos are a genus of four species occurring in Africa, Asia and southern Europe. They mainly victimize babblers, bulbuls and laughingthrushes, but the Great Spotted Cuckoo in southern Europe parasitizes Magpies, *Pica pica*.

Six genera within the Cuculinae subfamily each contain only a single species. In Africa there is the rare Thick-billed Cuckoo, *Pachycoccyx audeberti*, which is known to parasitize only one species – the Black Helmet Shrike, *Prionops retzii*. Three monotypic genera occur in New Guinea but they have been little studied, and their breeding habits remain undocumented. They include the Black-capped Cuckoo,

Table 2 *Distributions, habitats and main hosts of parasitic cuckoos, Cuculinae*

Group	No. species Total = 47	Breeding region	T = tropical P = Palaearctic A = Australasian	Main habitat	Main hosts
Cuculus clamosus, gularis, solitarius	3	Africa	T	Woodland	Shrikes, chats
canorus, fugax, micropterus, poliocephalus, saturatus, sparverioides	6	Eurasia, Madagascar	T & P	Woodland	Warblers, pipits, chats (insectivorous passerines)
vagans, varius	2	SE Asia	T	Forest	Babblers
pallidus	1	Australia	A	Savanna Woodland	Honeyeaters
Cacomantis merulinus, sonneratii	2	SE Asia	T	Open woods and forests	Warblers, bulbuls, babblers
variolosus, castaneiventris heinrichi, pyrrhophaneus	4	New Guinea, Indonesia – Australia	T	Forest	Warblers, imperfectly known
Chrysococcyx caprius, cupreus, klaas, flavigularis	4	Africa	T	Forest & savanna	Weavers, sunbirds

Cercococcyx mechowi, montanus, olivinus	3	Africa	T	Dense forest	Unknown
Eudynamis scolopacea	1	SE Asia – Australia	T	Woodland	Crows
taitensis	1	New Zealand	A	Forest	Warblers
Clamator coromondus	1	SE Asia	T	Forest & savanna	Laughingthrushes
glandarius	1	S Europe – Africa	T & P	Forest & savanna	Crows
levaillanti	1	Africa	T	Forest & savanna	Babblers
jacobinus	1	Africa – SE Asia	T	Forest & savanna	Bubuls, babblers, Laughingthrushes
Rhamphomantis, Caliechthrus, Microdynamis	3	New Guinea	T	Forest & forest edge	Unknown
Scythrops novaehollandiae	1	Indonesia – Australia	T	Woodland	Crows
Surniculus lugubris	1	SE Asia	T	Forest & scrub	Drongos, babblers
Pachycocyx audeberti	1	Africa	T	Forest	Shrikes

Microdynamis parva, the Little Long-billed Cuckoo, *Rhamphomantis megarhynchus*, and the White-crowned Koel, *Caliechthrus leucolophus*.

The Drongo Cuckoo, *Surniculus lugubris*, occurs in India and south-east Asia where it parasitizes a variety of songbirds, particularly the Black Drongo, *Dicrurus macrocercus*, which the cuckoo resembles by having a black plumage and partly forked tail. Perhaps most spectacular in the parasitic group, however, is the Channel-billed Cuckoo, *Scythrops novaehollandiae*, occurring from the islands of tropical south-east Asia to northern and eastern Australia. Compared to the tiny glossy cuckoos this is a large, heavily-billed and noisy bird which parasitizes crows and others. Like the Koel and Great Spotted Cuckoo, the female Channel-bill lays several eggs per host nest and the young do not eject their nest-mates.

Non-parasitic cuckoos (Phaenicophinae)

This subfamily contains 28 species in five genera found mainly in the New World, but also in south-east Asia and Africa. The most studied is the *Coccyzus* group, with eight species in the New World. Most of these live in the tropics of Central and South America, but two species migrate to and breed in North America. The Yellow- and Black-billed Cuckoos (*Coccyzus americanus* and *C. erythropthalmus*) are the New World counterparts of the Old World parasitic cuckoos. In their appearance, habits, calls, diets, migrations and dispersion, these North American cuckoos are not too dissimilar from the *Cuculus* cuckoos of the Palaeartic (Table 3). Yet their breeding habits are totally opposite. The Yellow- and Black-billed Cuckoos build flimsy nests of small twigs and roots in which they lay about four pale blue or green eggs at intervals of two or more days. Both parents share the incubation of the eggs and feeding of the young on a diet of caterpillars and grasshoppers. The young leave the nest very early at only 7–8 days old although they cannot fly for a further fortnight.

Perhaps the most exciting aspect of these North American cuckoos, although it has received very little attention, is the occasional parasitic behaviour which, as discussed earlier, led Darwin (1859) to suggest that these cuckoos were travelling the same road to parasitism as the European Cuckoo. The list of species known to have received eggs of these cuckoos is not long (Table 4), and the majority of records refer to cases of intra-specific parasitism between the two species. The phenomenon is difficult to study for obvious reasons but recently Nolan and Thompson (1975) found that instances of parasitism by Yellow-billed Cuckoos in southern Indiana increased during years of super-abundant food. Good food supplies enabled the birds to produce more eggs than usual, so that

Appearance		
length	28cm	33cm
weight	c. 60g	c. 110g
profile	Hawk-like in flight	Hawk-like
colour	Brown and white	Grey and white
Migration	From tropical South America; nocturnal; arrives in breeding range April/May, departs Sept/Oct; males arrive before females	From tropical Africa; nocturnal; arrives April/May, departs July/Aug; males before females
Feeding		
main diet	Caterpillars (especially colonial), grasshoppers, bugs	Caterpillars (especially hairy ones)
hunting strategy	Wait and watch, or exploit colony	Wait and watch, or gorge colony
Calls	A variety of different bubbling calls, oft repeated	Males have 'cuck-oo', oft repeated; females with distinctive bubbling note
Breeding habits		
nest	Flimsy structure of sticks placed in bush, sparsely lined with leaves	None, but wide range of nest-types in different host species
Eggs		
egg-size	c. 27 × 22mm	c. 22 × 16mm
egg-weight	c. 6-8g	3-4g
egg-colour	Pale blue	Polymorphic
shell	Thin, fragile	Thick, strong
number eggs laid	2-7 in clutch, maybe double brooded	Usually 10-15 (up to 25)
laying interval	2 days	2 days
egg-weight as proportion of body weight	c. 12%	2.75%
incubation period	10-11 days	11-12 days
Young		
at birth	Blind, black skin, white stiff down; able to support own weight (c. 9g)	Blind, pink skin, naked; able to eject nest-mates, weight c. 4g
weight at 7 days old	c.35g	c.35g
gape colour	Bright red, white spots	Bright orange red
age leave nest	7-8 days	21 days

Table 4   *List of species in the nests of which have been found eggs of North American* Coccyzus *cuckoos*

Species	Source
American Robin, *Turdus migratorius*	Bent 1940
Catbird, *Dumetella carolinensis*	Bent 1940
Dickcissel, *Spiza americana*	H. P. Attwater in Bent 1940
Black-throated Sparrow, *Amphispiza bilineata*	H. P. Attwater in Bent 1940
Wood Thrush, *Hylocichla mustelina*	Bendire 1895 in Bent 1940
Cedar Waxwing, *Bombycilla cedrorum*	Bendire 1895 in Bent 1940
Cardinal, *Richmondena cardinalis*	Bendire 1895 in Bent 1940
Chipping Sparrow, *Spizella passerina*	Bent 1940
Yellow Warbler, *Dendroica petechia*	Bent 1940
Wood Pewee, *Contopus virens*	Bent 1940
Rufous-sided Towhee, *Pipilo erythopthalmus*	Nolan & Thompson 1975

clutch-sizes increased and additional eggs were laid in other nests. These authors suggested that the erratic laying behaviour found in North American *Coccyzus* cuckoos could be attributed to irregular abundance of food with an associated breakdown of the normal stages of breeding in some females. This, they have proposed, may have been the antecedent of obligate brood parasitism in parasitic cuckoos. The possibility that a detailed comparison between American cuckoos and parasitic Old World cuckoos might reveal some hitherto hidden clues on the evolution of brood parasitism is therefore of great interest.

The *Piaya* genus of five species of non-parasitic cuckoos occurs in Central America where the best known among them is the Squirrel Cuckoo, *Piaya cayana*. A poor nest-building ability by an individual of this species was described by Skutch (1966) who watched a female attempting to position nesting material on an imaginary branch in a tall mango tree. The material simply fell to the ground some 12m below. After a week of such behaviour the female actually laid an egg into her imaginary nest: this also fell to the ground and smashed. As its name suggests, the Squirrel Cuckoo flies little, preferring to hop and clamber through trees in its rapid search for food. In contrast, two species of lizard cuckoos in the genus *Saurothera* spend most of their time on the ground searching for reptiles. They live on islands in the Carribean.

In the Old World the subfamily is represented by two genera. In India and south-east Asia a genus of 12 species of malcohas (*Phaenicophaeus*) are noted for their skulking behaviour in dense forests through which they are adept climbers, seldom flying into the open. They build untidy, dove-like nests of twigs in forest shrubs and both sexes share incubation of the two or three chalky-white eggs. Finally, the only genus of this subfamily in Africa is solely represented by the Yellowbill or Green Coucal, *Ceuthmochares aereus*. This is another skulking species inhabiting the thick cover of tropical rain forests where it has been little studied.

Ground cuckoos (Neomorphinae)

This group contains the roadrunners (*Geococcyx*) and other terrestrial cuckoos which move swiftly over the ground and rarely take to the air. It is a complex subfamily, with five genera in the New World and one (*Carpococcyx*) in south-east Asia. Furthermore, there are three species in two of the genera which are parasitic like the Cuculinae. The Striped Cuckoo, *Tapera naevia*, of Central and South America parasitizes small passerines, such as the Rufous-and-White Wren, *Thryothorus rufalbus*, or the Pale-breasted Spinetail, *Synallaxis albescens*. The nestling cuckoo is equipped with small hooks on the tip of its bill with which it kills the host's young when their heads are raised. The other parasitic genus, *Dromococcyx*, contains two South American species which are known to parasitize mainly flycatchers (Tyrannidae) but otherwise have not been studied. The *Neomorphus* genus of five species also occurs in South America, while the remaining genus in this subfamily is singly represented by the Lesser Ground Cuckoo, (*Morococcyx erythropygus*) found in Central America where it feeds and nests in open, semi-arid country.

The Roadrunner, *Geococcyx californianus*, is the most famous of this group. It lives in dry areas of Central and southern North America where it is largely territorial and sedentary. It rarely takes flight, preferring to outrun its enemies. The breeding season of the Roadrunner has a bimodal pattern (laying in April and again in late July), coinciding with the seasonal rains and associated abundance of lizards. In Arizona, nests are usually built in desert cactus plants and 2–7 eggs are laid in a clutch (Ohmart 1973). As in the American *Coccyzus* cuckoos, larger clutches are laid at times of greater food availability. There is even a record of a Roadrunner's egg found in the nest of a raven (Pemberton 1925). The young hatch asynchronously so that if the food supply diminishes for some reason, the youngest in the brood may be eaten by their parents.

Anis and Guira (Crotophaginae)

These Central and South American birds exhibit further peculiar breeding habits within the cuckoo family. They are gregarious to the extent of building communal nests in which several females lay their eggs and share responsibilities of incubation and tending young. The males also help. Each group or colony of anis owns a territory in which a bulky nest is built in a tree. The large eggs are pale blue when laid but quickly become covered with a thick chalky deposit. They are laid at varying intervals according to the dominance of each hen. In the Groove-billed Ani, *Crotophaga sulcirostris*, the dominant female removes eggs laid by the others prior to laying her own so that the final clutch contains mainly her eggs (Vehrencamp 1976). In general anis feed in small flocks of up to 20 birds on terrestrial insects, especially those flushed by grazing animals or columns of army ants.

The Guira Cuckoo, *Guira guira*, is found in tropical Brazil and Argentina and is considered the most primitive member of the subfamily. The birds spend most of the year in flocks but tend to separate into breeding pairs within an overall group territory. Defence of these individual nesting territories, however, is not vigorous, resulting in much intrusion and occasional shared nests.

Davis (1942) presented strong evidence of an evolutionary development of this social nesting system in the Crotophaginae, from the primitive Guira to the advanced Smooth-billed Ani. The main factor involved in this development, he suggested, was a modification of territorialism (Table 5), but many other factors (including unequal sex-ratios, poor incubation behaviour and care of young, a continuous moult, and a mainly grassland habitat with only scattered clumps of trees suitable for roosting and nesting), may have been contributory. Communal nesting in this group represents an offshoot of peculiar breeding habits within the whole cuckoo family, not, as has been suggested, a stage in the development of brood parasitism such as is found in the Cuculinae (Davis 1942).

Coucals (Centropodinae)

This subfamily contains a single genus with about 25 species distributed throughout the Old World tropics. Their main distinguishing feature is a straight hindclaw from which they are sometimes called lark-heeled cuckoos. The legs are long and the wings short and rounded, indicating a largely terrestrial lifestyle. Indeed they feed mainly on the ground on large insects or small animals. The nest is usually an untidy, rather globular structure made of grasses and small twigs and lined with leaves. Both sexes build the nest, usually above the ground in thick cover or thorny bush. Normally 2–4 eggs are laid which are white with a thick, chalky surface and incubated by both sexes. As in other non-parasitic cuckoos, the young hatch at irregular intervals and have black skins covered with white, wiry down. The African White-browed Coucal, *Centropus superciliosus*, is reported to carry its young away from danger by holding them between its legs, while Vernon (1971) found that young Black Coucals, *C. grillii*, produced a defensive snake-like hiss when

1 Film-maker Maurice Tibbles setting up his camera before entering a hide while making the BBC film, *The Private Life of The Cuckoo*. He spent many eight-hour sessions in hides waiting for a female Cuckoo to arrive at a nest

2 The author about to enter a hide strategically placed near a Reed Warbler's nest that is expected to be visited by a Cuckoo

3 Part of the study site at St Ives, Cambridgeshire alongside a disused railwayline

4 One of the young Cuckoos (code name 75N) wing-tagged during the study

5 The first male Cuckoo caught on 24 April 1975 by enticing it into a mist-net with tape recordings of Cuckoo calls. This bird was showing signs of body moult

6 The similarity in appearance between Cuckoo (top) and Sparrowhawk, *Accipiter nisus*. Hawk-mimicry by the Cuckoo may protect it against raptors

7 A female Reed Warbler brooding her clutch containing three of her own eggs and one of a Cuckoo

8 A female Cuckoo watches a reedbed for signs of Reed Warblers building their nests. By sitting quietly and unobtrusively like this for up to several hours, the Cuckoo is soon ignored by the hosts who continue their normal activities

9 and **10** Female Cuckoo robbing the eggs from a nest which she does not intend to parasitize. This may provide food, or prevent rival female Cuckoos using the same area, or cause the hosts to build a new nest which may be parasitized later

11 The eggs robbed in this way are normally swallowed whole at the nest. The Cuckoo leaves the nest empty

12 Another female Cuckoo robbing a Reed Warbler's nest by eating all the eggs

13 A Willow Warbler *Phylloscopus trochilus* attacking the head of a Cuckoo placed near its nest. Such vigorous defence of the nest may deter the Cuckoo from parasitizing this potential host species. *Photo: Eric Hosking*

Table 5 *Phylogeny of social nesting behaviour in Crotophaginae*
(from Davis 1942)

Genus	Species	Region	Pairing and territorial system
Guira	*guira* Guira Cuckoo	Tropical South America – Brazil & Argentina	Pairs nesting alone within an overall colonial territory. Defence of pair or colonial territory not vigorous. Some nests shared.
Crotophaga	*major* Greater Ani	N Argentina, Brazil & Panama	Colony composed of monogamous pairs which unite to defend (not vigorously) the whole territory in which one nest is built.
	sulcirostris Groove-billed Ani	N Peru, Central America & Texas	Colony of about 2 or 3 (rarely more) pairs co-operate to build one nest which is vigorously defended.
	ani Smooth-billed Ani	N Argentina to Yucatan, Florida & West Indies	Colony comprised of promiscuous individuals producing one nest which is aggressively defended against intruders.

disturbed, plus foul-smelling faeces if handled, and left the nest when only 11 days old.

Couas (Couinae)
The Couinae subfamily contains nine or ten species (*Coua delalandei* may now be extinct) in a single genus confined to Madagascar. The birds are non-migratory and poorly known, this summary being an abstract from Rand's (1936) paper following a French-Anglo-American expedition to Madagascar in 1929–1931.

Couas apparently feed on large insects such as grasshoppers and caterpillars, like other cuckoos, but they also consume fruits and small reptiles (e.g. chameleons). Three species (*C. caerula*, *C. cristata*, and *C. verrauxi*) are mainly arboreal forest-dwelling birds which hop, run and 'bounce' off branches as they progress through the trees. They have a heavy, laboured flight, preferring to glide from tree to tree, and have loud harsh calls producing characteristic forest noises. The Crested Coua, *C. cristata*, commonly calls at sunset, forming a loud chorus with its neighbours. These forest couas are generally found in pairs, but occasionally in small parties of three to five.

The other seven species are largely terrestrial birds of semi-arid scrub, forest-edge brush or dry forests. These are mainly solitary except in the breeding season when they have harsh loud calls uttered from a low perch. The Running Coua, *C. cursor*, usually walks sedately on the ground in search of food, but can run at great speed when alarmed.

To summarize the breeding habits of the cuckoo family: firstly there are the terrestrial forms such as the Lesser Ground Cuckoo, which build an open-bowl nest of leaves and sticks on the ground usually under cover. Secondly, the coucals build untidy but distinctive oval-shaped nests of grass with a neatly lined cup of leaves. Next, the more arboreal non-parasitic cuckoos build flimsy nests of sticks, while the Crotophaginae build bulky domed communal nests also of sticks in trees. Finally, the brood parasites build no nests and are totally dependent upon other species.

Notably missing in these nesting strategies is one whereby a nest built by another species is appropriated by a cuckoo and used to rear its own young. This is a common practice in many birds, and one which has been supposed to lead eventually to full parasitism. While it is not apparent in any of today's cuckoos, it is found in the parasitic cowbird group where the South American Bay-winged Cowbird steals the nest of another species or occasionally builds its own nest in which it rears its young.

The eggs of members of the cuckoo family show extremes in egg-weight to body-weight ratio; an egg of the European Cuckoo, for example, weighs less than 3 per cent of the weight of a breeding female, in contrast to an ani's egg weighing 20–25 per cent of the body weight (Lack 1968). In general the eggs of parasitic cuckoos are small in proportion to body size whereas non-parasitic cuckoo eggs are proportionally large (see Chapter 9). The former are also thick-shelled and polymorphic in colour compared to the latter which are thin-shelled and unmarked white, blue or green. Young of the nesting species hatch in an advanced state with dark skins covered with stiff down; they develop rapidly and fledge prematurely. Young parasitic cuckoos hatch naked and leave their host's nest only when able to fly. Incubation periods are remarkably short even in non-parasitic species, suggesting that rapid embryonic development was a cuckoo feature prior to the evolution of brood parasitism. For the parasites, early hatching gives the young a competitive advantage over the host's young, while in nesting species it may be an advantage to hatch and leave the nest as quickly as possible to avoid predation or to exploit a constantly changing food resource.

Young parasitic cuckoos reared by hosts smaller than themselves increase in weight at about the same rate as the complete host's brood would have, but usually take longer to fledge (see Chapter 10). Those which are raised with larger hosts generally fledge earlier than their host young. On reaching independence, young parasitic cuckoos dissociate from their foster parents, often migrating to their winter quarters alone and perhaps several weeks after their actual parents.

Characteristics

Appearance

All cuckoos, whether parasitic or not, are characterized by having zygodactyl feet: the first and fourth toes are directed backwards, the second and third forwards. This arrangement in birds is better known in parrots (Psittacidae) and woodpeckers (Picadae) where it is a special adaptation for climbing. A climbing ability is apparent in the adults of several cuckoos (e.g. the malcohas), and in others it is restricted to the young. A young American Black-billed Cuckoo, *Coccyzus erythropthalmus*, for example, leaves the nest at only a week old, but is able to cling from a perch by a single toe from only a few hours. It maintains a climbing stage for at least a further two weeks before it can fly (Herrick 1910). Perhaps this premature departure from the nest has survival value similar to the rapid dispersal of nidifugous birds. Most young parasitic cuckoos are already dispersed in the environment by their parents' habit of laying only one egg in each host nest. In these young there is no climbing stage, other than an ability to eject the host's young over the side of the nest, and they remain in the nest until they can fly. Nonetheless, they do have to cling on to some rather precarious nests at times. In adult cuckoos the zygodactyl feet are probably useful when balancing in delicate foliage where many of them feed.

In size the Cuculidae range from a mere 16cm (sparrow-size) to around 60cm (crow-size), the European Cuckoo falling in the middle of the range at about 33cm. The smallest cuckoos are found in *Chrysococcyx* and *Cacomantis* weighing as little as 20g in some species, whereas at the other extreme, the Roadrunner measures some 56cm and weighs about 300g, and the Channel-billed Cuckoo reaches 60cm and is even heavier.

Cuckoos have medium to long wings, pointed in the case of

long-distance migrants, rounded in more sedentary species. In flight they vary from swift, sharp-winged migrants through round-winged and weak-flying arboreal and semi-terrestrial species, to the highly terrestrial ground cuckoos which only fly under extreme provocation.

Tails are usually long in proportion to body size and are graduated, with normally ten feathers decreasing in length from the inner pair outwards. The sides or tips of the feathers are often marked with conspicuous white spots or notches. With long, slightly fanned tails and rather slender, elongated bodies, many species seem larger than they actually are (see Mimicry below).

The bill is slightly decurved in all species, often with a more or less hooked tip and with rounded, somewhat prominent nostrils situated at the base. Coucals, anis and the Channel-bill have heavy bills. Large, bright-coloured gapes are common, particularly in young parasitic cuckoos. Lack (1968) proposed that the huge gape, loud begging calls, and bright buccal colouring in the juvenile European Cuckoo act as a 'super-stimulus' to increase parental response in the hosts. The young of brood parasitic widowbirds finches in Africa have mimetic mouth patterns similar to the young of their particular host species and it has been shown experimentally that the hosts will only feed young with the 'right' pattern (Nicolai 1974). No such development occurs in parasitic cuckoos, but in the few species where young are raised with the host young (e.g. Koel and Great Spotted Cuckoo) the young parasites apparently mimic the appearance and calls of their foster siblings. Conspicuous and distinctive mouth markings also occur in many non-parasitic cuckoos.

Inconspicuous plumages and lack of ornamental feathers or brightly-coloured parts prevail in parasitic cuckoos, with the exception of the glossy *Chrysococcyx* genus. Some of the males of this group have bright metallic plumages of green, brown or purple, which are highly conspicuous when the birds are in the open but in the tropical forests where most of them live they are difficult to see. By assigning values of conspicuousness to various morphological features of all cuckoo genera, Payne (1967) demonstrated that parasitic cuckoos are considerably less conspicuous than their non-parasitic relatives. Presumably, therefore, dullness is an adaptation to avoid detection by hosts. In support of this theory, female parasitic cuckoos are usually cryptically coloured, and behave secretively near a host nest. They are also sometimes polymorphic (i.e. with different colour phases). Polymorphism in parasitic cuckoos parallels that found in raptors, particularly predators of small birds in which the juvenile and adult plumages differ. Payne (1967) suggested that the host species developed an image of a single morph, so that polymorphism helps to offset recognition. Examples include *Clamator* species in Africa with colour phases in different habitats, and female *Chrysococcyx* with plumages ranging from bright green to dull brown. Polymorphism has not been recorded in non-parasitic cuckoos.

Mimicry
The above characteristics of appearance in cuckoos lead to the question of mimicry in the parasitic species. It has long been noted that some parasitic cuckoos show a close resemblance to some other bird: either to their respective hosts or to birds of prey. The European Cuckoo, for example, appears to mimic the Sparrowhawk, *Accipiter nisus*, the resemblance leading to the old belief that Cuckoos turned into Sparrowhawks in winter. The rarer brown (hepatic) phase found only in the females apparently mimics the Kestrel, *Falco tinnunculus*. Other *Cuculus* cuckoos also seem to mimic the common hawks in their areas – the Indian hawk-cuckoos *Cuculus varius* and *C. sparverioides*, as their names suggest, look like the Shikra and Besra Sparrowhawks, *Accipiter badius* and *A. virgatus* respectively.

Of those parasitic cuckoos which seem to mimic their hosts, the Koel has a black plumage similar to the House Crow, so when the adult crows drive the black male Koel away from their nest, the brown, spotted female can lay unmolested. For this to work satisfactorily, these cuckoos have to form more than transitory pair-bonds. Also in India, the Drongo Cuckoo, with its glossy black plumage, forked tail and similar posture, looks and acts like one of its hosts, the Black Drongo. By mimicking the host, Drongo Cuckoos are able to successfully parasitize these pugnacious and strongly territorial birds, in the same way that the Koel parasitizes the House Crow.

Mimicry by a defenceless or palatable animal to an offensive or unpalatable one is known as aggressive mimicry. The evidence points to such a condition in some of the parasitic cuckoos. The most generally proposed view is that such aggressive mimicry is directed at the hosts in order to facilitate nest parasitism. There is no conclusive evidence in favour of this. It has been assumed that a hawk-like appearance intimidates small birds which may be temporarily alarmed from their nests or territories. However, it is well known from field observations that cuckoos elicit attacks or mobbing reactions from small birds; in other words, they do not scare them away. Experiments using stuffed cuckoos and models near the nests of potential hosts have shown that some birds readily distinguish between parasite and predator (Edwards *et al.* 1949, 1950; Smith and Hosking 1955). In the Willow Warbler, *Phylloscopus trochilus*, (an infrequent host of European Cuckoos), the introduction of a stuffed cuckoo near the nest resulted in an immediate attack by the owners while the presentation of a stuffed sparrowhawk produced fear reactions such as the 'hewie' alarm note and the birds would not approach their nest but flitted around at a distance. In the Nightingale, *Luscinia megarhynchos* (a very rare host), stuffed specimens of both Cuckoo and sparrowhawk placed near a nest produced violent attacks.

Similar, though more detailed, experiments with models of parasitic cowbirds in America showed that, in general, the amount of host aggression was proportional to the degree of parasitism on each species, the regular hosts attacking most strongly (Robertson and Morgan 1976). Since cowbirds are not mimics of their hosts or of birds of prey, it appears that hosts recognize them for what they are, or at least as threats to the survival of their eggs. The overall inference from these experiments on host-parasite interactions is that regularly parasitized birds identify their parasites and try to defend their nests with appropriate action (see Chapter 7). The supposed hawk-mimicry of European Cuckoos did not seem to frighten hosts at all, although a stuffed cuckoo is not as hawk-like as a flying live one.

An alternative explanation for mimicry of a hawk (or aggressive species in the case of the Koel and Drongo Cuckoo) has recently been emphasized by Ward (1979). He suggested that the cuckoos are using a bluff to avoid predation by larger raptors. A hawk might not be so eager to attack a cuckoo if it thought its quarry could be a more powerfully equipped bird. Mimicry for this purpose would be beneficial to the cuckoo all the year round and to both sexes, whereas mimicry for frightening the hosts would be useful only to the female and for just a few weeks of the year. Also in favour of this explanation, cuckoos spend most of their time in the tropics where they are potential prey to a larger number of predatory birds than elsewhere. Their habits also make them particularly susceptible to predation by raptors at times: they are mostly solitary, occupying exposed perches, sometimes feeding in the open, and having presence-revealing calls. In spite of this, Cuckoos sometimes fall prey to sparrowhawks and other raptors in Britain (see Chapter 4).

The subject requires further critical study. Another possibility is that the similarity between parasitic cuckoos and their models has arisen, not through mimicry, but through chance evolution of two groups. In this context the North American cuckoos are of some interest: they are not parasitic and their plumages do not resemble birds of prey, but they are attributed with having a hawk-like profile. While it is of great interest that cuckoos resemble hawks, there are other birds which in their turn resemble cuckoos. These include the Cuckoo-falcon, *Aviceda cuculoides*, cuckoo-shrikes (Campephagidae) and cuckoo-doves *Macropygia* (Columbidae), all of which have barred underparts like the Cuckoo.

Diets
Cuckoos are universally renowned for consuming hairy, warningly-coloured and often toxic caterpillars, chiefly the larvae of butterflies and moths (lepidoptera). Many caterpillars have special colours or colonial habits to advertise their unpalatability to predators. By a combination of visual and taste senses, a predator soon learns which are inedible and rejects them. Cuckoos, however, not only eat these caterpillars without ill-effects, they eat them in very large quantities to the exclusion of other foods, occasionally congregating in localities where there are periodic caterpillar outbreaks. Other birds largely avoid such foods.

Where they are known the diets of each cuckoo subfamily seem correlated with the peculiar breeding habits in the groups as discussed earlier. In almost every group a link can be established between sporadic food supplies and strange breeding behaviour. Thus the Cuculinae feed on hairy caterpillars and are all parasitic; the Phaenicophinae also feed on sporadic caterpillars but nest normally, only occasionally parasitizing each others' and other birds' nests; the Neomorphinae contain three parasitic species, while the Roadrunner breeds in response to twice-yearly abundances of insect and reptilian food; and the Crotophaginae feed on ground insects flushed by grazing animals or army ants and nest communally.

Two species, the Koel and the Channel-bill, feed almost exclusively on fruits, even poisonous ones at times. Other cuckoos also take fruits occasionally but large insects are by far the most common foods. Besides caterpillars, these include grasshoppers, termites, ants, stick insects, bugs, beetles and many others. Some species (e.g. the lizard cuckoos) specialize on reptiles, including even poisonous snakes. Others occasionally prey on small animals and young birds, and many cuckoos, irrespective of breeding habits, are known to eat the eggs of other birds. This habit seems to be restricted to the females only and is probably connected with their own egg-production requirements (see Chapter 4).

Vocalizations
Nearly all cuckoos have loud, distinctive and oft-repeated calls by which they can usually be identified. Very often the calls or song are the only indication that the species concerned is present in an area, especially in tropical forests. They are generally only heard in the breeding season. The calls are far-carrying, probably to allow intraspecific distinction

where several sparse, related species live in the same region (e.g. in Japan) (Lack 1968). They also serve to attract mates which are likely to be thinly dispersed. In some species the calls are frequently used at night, thus drawing further attention to the birds. Single, double or treble syllable calls are most common. Various people have remarked upon the somewhat ventriloquial effect of cuckoo calls: this is undoubtedly caused by a bird turning in different directions on its song-perch.

The preceding characteristics and breeding habits of the world's cuckoos are intended as an introduction to the more detailed examination of the European Cuckoo which follows in subsequent chapters. I have attempted to include any interesting points about other cuckoos where they relate to some aspect of the life and behaviour of the European Cuckoo.

2 | The European Cuckoo

With such a widespread breeding distribution (Figure 1), the Cuckoo is obviously not a rare bird in terms of overall population level, but exact numbers are difficult to assess by the various census methods available for bird counts. A recent survey of breeding birds in the British Isles (Sharrock 1976) revealed that Cuckoos were recorded in 91 per cent of the 10km squares in Britain and Ireland. A rough estimate of 5–10 pairs per 10km square gave a total of up to 35,000 pairs. Local counts in Britain during the last 20 years by the Common Birds Census organized by the British Trust for Ornithology show little change in Cuckoo numbers in either farmland or woodland, the two main habitats surveyed. However, a widespread decline was recorded in most areas of Britain following the increased use of insecticides in the 1950s (Parslow 1973). With the withdrawal of certain harmful pesticides in recent years, Cuckoo numbers in Britain, at least, seem to have stabilized, although they may still be under pressure from habitat destruction and the associated loss of caterpillars and hosts.

Appearance

Few people in Europe can be unfamiliar with the Cuckoo since it readily announces its presence in the spring and summer throughout the region. While its call is distinctive, the bird itself is difficult to observe and many a determined effort to see one is unsuccessful. There are several reasons for this.

Firstly the Cuckoo is predominantly grey in colour and surprisingly well-camouflaged in a variety of situations. A slate-grey upper surface is a good match to the grey rocks of mountain habitats, whereas in woodland the grey bib and white barred underparts are 'disruptive' in foliage. When a Cuckoo settles on a dead branch or exposed post its general drab appearance is quite inconspicuous. This attitude is commonly adopted by a bird surveying the environment for food or host nests. The wings hang low so that they effectively cover the paler underparts, making the

Cuckoo even more difficult to see. As discussed in the last chapter, there is good reason to remain unnoticed: its hawk-like appearance, whether mimicry or not, has the effect of illiciting attack or mobbing reactions from many birds. If these attacks become violent the Cuckoo is forced to take cover or move away. It is also inconspicuous in flight. Often a bird will fly very close to the ground, maybe only a few centimetres above the ground vegetation. They also use depressions in the terrain, ditches, walls, hedges and other cover to avoid detection. Many times I have been annoyed by a Cuckoo's ability to fly away from a bush, keeping that bush directly in line between itself and the observer. Its dull appearance is again of benefit in flight. The wings are barely raised above the horizontal line of the body, thus concealing the paler underparts. In the way it flies and its use of cover it is again reminiscent of the Sparrowhawk.

Much of the time Cuckoos stay either in dense foliage, or remain motionless on an exposed perch. On other occasions, when wishing to advertise their presence, they become very conspicuous despite their dull appearance. In open country favoured perches include exposed wires and prominent posts; these are especially used by the males when singing. On such places and with loud attractive songs Cuckoos are highly noticeable, as they lower their wings and fan their tails, revealing a striking pattern. A special flight of the male can also render the bird conspicuous: it makes a rather slow flapping flight, even singing as it goes. This is especially apparent during the courtship period in late April and early May. The female at this time of year may also travel fairly openly as it investigates different males and explores the local landscape. It may utter the bubbling call in flight when courted by a male, and it is not unusual to see a female being chased by two or more males at once. At this time of year, Cuckoos tend to be most conspicuous at dawn and dusk presumably because they are spending most of the day quietly feeding. However, they are somewhat unpredictable and one can never guarantee seeing a Cuckoo at any time of day.

There are thus no clear rules for the keen Cuckoo-watcher. Ideally one needs to locate a breeding site or a good feeding place and, playing the bird at its own game, simply sit and wait. They are, on the other hand, not very exciting birds to watch: they seem to spend hours doing nothing, only to move just at the moment your are distracted by something more interesting. A male will sit for hours occasionally singing and preening, while a female remains quiet and still when searching for host nests. To be sure of observing a Cuckoo in the process of parasitizing a nest, one needs to have an intimate knowledge of all the host nests within the Cuckoo's range, and to know the egg-laying pattern of the particular Cuckoo. Without this information, which clearly involves a lot of field work, any sighting of a Cuckoo laying its egg is bound to be a rare chance event. Generally though, if a bird is seen gliding around a small area in the afternoon or evening sometime between late May and early July, it is likely to be about to lay in a nearby nest and if the intended nest can be found in time, it will be possible to witness the event at very close range since the bird will not be put off by a hide placed nearby at quite late notice.

Another good place to see Cuckoos is at recognized feeding places where there are plenty of caterpillars. These include hedges, woodland rides, patches of heather, areas of scrub, reedbeds, disused railway lines, or anywhere else where caterpillars are concentrated. The use of any one place is temporary, depending on the availability of food. Sometimes it may be possible to arrange a prominent post in such a feeding site, and this will be readily used by Cuckoos. Often, several birds may be seen together at the same place.

Individual Cuckoos vary enormously in their shyness of human observers. One particular female at my study site in 1978 and 1979 was especially shy and evasive, and I rarely saw it occupy an exposed position. I found 15 eggs laid by this bird in both seasons, yet I only witnessed a laying on two occasions and the total number of observations numbered a mere dozen or so. Another bird which I first encountered in 1979 was not at all concerned about human presence and I saw it almost every day during the laying period, when it also produced 15 eggs.

Plumage

There are certain aspects of the plumage of Cuckoos which are worthy of comment. Most book descriptions and illustrations suggest that the male and female can be distinguished by the female having more brown or brown-tinged feathers on the otherwise grey bib. In the field this is not often apparent and there are many females (most, in my experience) which look exactly like males and lack any brown breast feathers, as some of the photographs in this book show. On the other hand, some females are browner and smaller than males and can be distinguished with ease in the field. At the extreme a few females are totally brown and quite unlike males or other females: these are regarded as hepatic colour phases or morphs. They are relatively rare with no equivalent in males. Voipio (1953) assumed that hawk-mimicry was responsible for producing relatively more hepatic females in woodland habitats where the local host species would (he thought) be more aggressive towards Sparrowhawks and, therefore, grey-phase Cuckoos. Grey Cuckoos would then be more common in open habitats where hosts would be more aggressive towards Kestrels and hepatic Cuckoos. This interpretation does not seem to have been borne out in Great Britain where grey Cuckoos are much the commonest type in all habitats. No quantitative data on this subject are available.

A young Cuckoo appears in one of three colour phases. These are rather variable but usually distinct. One has grey to grey-brown upperparts with varying degrees of brown feathers. The second type is more predominantly brown with dark bars to the feathers. Both types have most of the feathers of their upperparts tipped with white or buff-white. Underparts of the two groups are more or less the same with dull-white feathers heavily barred dark brown, the browner type having buffer tinged feathers and fewer bars on the chin and throat (Witherby, et al. 1938). The third type is the hepatic phase in the juvenile which is a rich chestnut, not so striking as in the adult, while the rump and tail coverts have few dark bars (Witherby, et al. 1938; Voipio 1953). This last author concluded that there was a gradual series from grey-brown to hepatic plumages in young Cuckoos, whereas adults were either grey or hepatic. He examined a small sample (28) of skins of young Cuckoos in the Helsinki Museum and found half were grey-brown, half were rufous. Of 18 that were sexed on their labels, again half were of each sex. Eight of the 9 males were grey-brown and only 1 was rufous, whereas 7 of the 9 females were rufous and only 2 were grey-brown. If these specimens were sexed by autopsy, this suggests that sexual dimorphism is manifest in Cuckoos at an early age (young birds can be categorized into these different colour types at about 12–14 days old).

Another feature of the plumage of young Cuckoos is the white patch of feathers on the back of the head. This varies somewhat in size but is present in nearly all young and readily distinguishes a bird of the year. In my opinion it is a signal to other birds, and could be further evidence in favour of hawk-mimicry in Cuckoos. The signal is not directed at the foster parents since they normally approach the young bird from the front, attracted by its loud begging calls and red gape. It is also not a signal to the young Cuckoo's own parents because they take no interest in their offspring and even migrate ahead of them. It could, therefore, be a signal to a bird of prey such as an *Accipiter* hawk where a similar white occipital patch occurs in both sexes and their young. The purpose of the white patch in hawks is not clear either, although in the male Sparrowhawk it is used as an appeasement gesture to the female (I. Newton, pers. comm.). It may have protection value therefore in reducing the chance of attack. As young Cuckoos are especially vulnerable to predation by raptors, mimicry of the white nape and of the brown barred plumage may thus have survival value, particularly in late summer, when the young hawks themselves leave the nest.

Finally on the subject of plumage in Cuckoos there is the question of moult. This is a problem because European Cuckoos replace most of their feathers in Africa in winter, so our knowledge of moult depends upon specimens collected in various parts of Africa. Various authors have examined the moult in Cuckoos in some detail and the serious student is referred to their works (Verheyen 1950; Stresemann & Stresemann 1961). Under normal conditions body moult in adults may start in late June or July, may be arrested during migration, then completed in Africa during November to March. Some adults returning to Europe in the spring may still be undergoing body moult. Replacement of the flight and tail feathers follows a similar pattern, some adults moulting a few primaries in Europe and completing the moult in Africa having stopped during the migration period. Primaries are not replaced sequentially, but rather in non-adjacent pairs. Thus primary numbers 9 and 4 are moulted simultaneously, numbers 7 and 1, 5 and 2, 8 and 3, then number 6, and finally 10. This has the effect that each moulting feather is always protected by a full-grown feather on each side, so there is no resulting loss of flight-power.

Young birds may also begin to moult in Europe and arrest their moult during migration. In its first winter the young Cuckoo undergoes a complete moult of body, tail and flight feathers into the grey adult plumage. Some birds retain a variable number of browner secondary and other wing feathers which distinguish them in the hand from older birds. Sparrowhawks can be aged by the retention of a few brown juvenile feathers in the same way, but these birds do not moult until the summer. Brühn (1960) kept a young Cuckoo over winter and found that it became emaciated during November to mid-December when moulting; it recovered in condition about mid-January and became restless at night, presumably in readiness for its migration.

Colour of the soft parts

While the general appearance is of a grey, well-camouflaged bird, the colours of the soft parts of a Cuckoo are bright but not conspicuous. The feet are yellow as in the Sparrowhawk, but in the Cuckoo the legs are very short and feathered so that only the toes are usually visible. The iris and orbital ring are also yellow but, again, these are not apparent from a distance. The eyelids are also yellow. Iris colour in juveniles and hepatic-phase females is hazel. In adults the bill is a dark horn above and greenish below, rather yellow near the base. The upper mandible has near its base two prominent, rounded nostrils but, unlike some other cuckoos, there are no rictal or nasal bristles. The flanges of the gape are also yellow while the interior buccal colour is a brilliant orange-red throughout a Cuckoo's life. In the nestling this may stimulate the hosts to feed it, but its function in adults is more obscure. The only time it seems to be shown is when a bird is mobbed by some harmless passerine. Under these circumstances a Cuckoo will occasionally expose its orange-red gape suddenly to the attacker. It may thus act as a defensive bluff. Such an interpretation could even be applied to the young Cuckoo: the gape colour serving as a warning colour to a predator.

Posture and movements

Cuckoos assume several different postures during various activities. Typically, from a distance the male appears 'banana-shaped' with its curved body and wings and slightly raised tail. Several postures and outline appearances of Cuckoos in flight are illustrated in Figure 2.

When feeding on the ground the Cuckoo, with its very short legs, moves in a series of awkward hops, as opposed to running or walking. It rarely moves far in this way, usually flying back to a suitable perch. In trees and bushes it moves rather clumsily, jumping from one perch to another using its wings and tail for balance. In flight, however, it is quite a graceful bird, travelling rather swiftly and directly. It often glides up to a perch after a flight. It seems likely that the female's gliding style of flight during laying is to keep the egg, which is in the oviduct ready for immediate extrusion, safe and intact. The gliding flight also simulates a hawk and this may benefit the laying female in reducing attack from neighbouring birds, not just the immediate hosts. Several observers (Pounds 1965; Gervis 1966; Jones 1967; Radford 1965) have commented upon the high degree of resemblance between a gliding Cuckoo and a Sparrowhawk. Most of the observed incidents resulted in a Cuckoo egg being laid in the nest of some open-habitat host such as a Meadow Pipit, so Ash (1965) suggested that this method was used more often by females in those habitats where there were fewer vantage places. Possibly it allows the female to slow her speed and scan for nests from the air. Radford (1965) even noted a juvenile Cuckoo gliding around with alternating rapid and slow wing-beats in an open habitat in late summer, and again remarked on the resemblance to a Sparrowhawk.

Another style of flight which is similar to the above hawk-like flight and makes a Cuckoo appear even more like a bird of prey is soaring, in

Figure 2. Postures of the Cuckoo. (a) upright, alert; (b) 'banana' shape
on telegraph line; (c) male display; (d) female prior to egg laying;
(e) normal flight; (f) flight silhouette

which a bird circles and rises to several hundred metres above the ground using outstretched wings and little flapping flight. This is used mainly during courtship.

Size measurements

For its apparent size a Cuckoo is surprisingly light in weight. In a recent analysis by Seel (1977a) of British birds caught during 1949–1972, adult males averaged 118g and adult females 107g. Seel showed that in April adults weighed on average 129g (10 males) and 112g (6 females) whereas during the main breeding period in June they averaged only 114g (n=20) and 106g (n=14) respectively. This weight loss was re-couped in July when males averaged 133g (n=7) and females 112g (n=4): hence birds weighed more or less the same in the departure month as in the arrival month, despite the fact that in April they had just completed a long migration while in July they should be about to embark on one. There is a danger in interpreting these results, however, for the records derived entirely from coastal bird observatories where birds were presumably on migration and therefore carrying varying amounts of fat depending on their ultimate destinations. Figure 3 gives some additional data for birds caught in Cambridgeshire during the arrival and pre-laying period during 1975–1980. Although the sample is small and comprises several years there is an apparent decrease in weight during the seven week period. In West Germany weights of 15

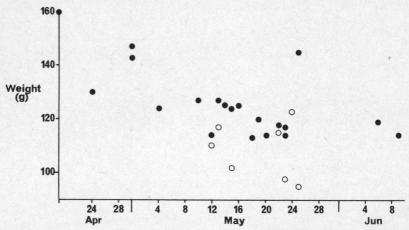

Figure 3. Weights of adult Cuckoos caught in Cambridgeshire, 1975–1980.
Closed circle = males, n = 20 range 113–160g, mean = 126g
Open circle = females, n = 7 range 95–122g, mean = 108.4g

adults caught in the breeding season averaged 117g (95–145, males and females combined), but birds in captivity fed on a suitable diet weighed 40–50 per cent more in late summer and autumn than in the spring (Löhrl 1979). Cuckoos possibly arrive at their breeding sites in spring with a small surplus of fat which can be used during food shortages. Caterpillars are not abundant in late April, particularly if the weather is cold, and observations of birds at this time of year suggest that they are feeding mainly on the ground, perhaps on terrestrial beetles (see Chapter 4).

Birds of the year in Britain had a lower body weight than adults (Seel 1977a). Of 151 records, the mean juvenile weight (both sexes) was only 92g, representing 18–31 per cent below the July weights of adults. Seel proposed that this difference necessitated a low rate of migration through Europe during which young birds increased in weight prior to migration to Africa. Lower body weight in juveniles, however, is commonly found in many species (e.g. raptors) and could be due to smaller general size and reduced wing-loading. Young Cuckoos being offered for sale in Italian bird markets are reported to be very fat. Adults presumably also fatten in southern Europe before migrating south.

Most bird identification books give the total length (bill-tip to tail-tip) for an adult Cuckoo as 330mm (13 inches). Bannerman (1955), however, recorded 380mm (15 inches) and, for Russian birds, Dement'ev et al. (1966) gave for males an average length of 360mm (range 322–395mm), and for females 336mm (range 310–360mm). Clearly this measurement can be extremely variable between and within sexes, and since it cannot be measured consistently by different workers and only from dead birds, it is of dubious value anyway. Females in the hand often seem smaller than males but, as with body weight, size is not a reliable indicator of sex. About half the total length of a Cuckoo is taken up by the tail.

Another measurement, wing-length, is also very variable in adult Cuckoos. Birds caught and measured alive in Britain between 1949 and 1972 averaged 218mm (standard deviation=10) for 136 males and 211mm (s.d.=7) for 78 females (Seel 1977a). Mean wing-lengths in Russia were 224mm and 212mm respectively (Dement'ev et al. 1966), indicating rather little east–west clinal variation. Adults caught in Cambridgeshire in 1975–1979 averaged 220mm (range 205–231mm) for 16 males and 208mm (range 200–220mm) for 6 females. All these results again show that males are larger on average than females but there is considerable overlap, so this criterion alone cannot be used for sex discrimination. The average wing-length of 173 juvenile Cuckoos recorded by Seel (1977a) was 197mm, much shorter than adults.

The legs of a Cuckoo are notably short (tarsi 18–24mm) (Witherby *et al.* 1938). This is in comparison with the similarly-sized male Sparrow-hawk which has relatively long tarsi (50–56mm) for striking and capturing its prey.

Subspecies of Cuculus canorus

Several subspecies of the nominate race *Cuculus canorus canorus* have been described for various parts of the Cuckoo's range. They are mostly confusing and in some doubt but are listed and described briefly in Table 6. Some are poorly defined.

Table 6 *Subspecies of Cuculus canorus (for distributions see figure 1)*

Subspecies and authority	Common name	Breeding range	
Cuculus canorus canorus Linneaus = *C.c. rumenicus* Tschusi and Dombrowski = *C.c. similis* Dombrowski	Common, European or Grey Cuckoo	Europe to western Siberia from N Russia and Scandinavia to Mediterranean area	Nominate race
Cuculus canorus bakeri Hartert	Khasia Hills Cuckoo	Assam, Burma and W China	Darker upperparts, broader black bars below further apart
Cuculus canorus bangsi Oberholser = *C.c. minor* A. E. Brehm	Iberian Cuckoo	Portugal, Spain and NW Africa	Smaller than nominate race
Cuculus canorus fallax Stresemann	Chinese Cuckoo	S China	Similar to *bakeri* but smaller
Cuculus canorus johanseni Tschusi = *C.c. maximus* Neumann		W Siberia to Lake Baikal	Paler, slightly larger and more narrowly barred
Cuculus canorus kleinschmidti Schiebel = ? *C.c. sardus* Trischitta	Corsican Cuckoo	Corsica, Sardinia	Darker upperparts
Cuculus canorus subtelephonus Zarundy = *C.c. kwenlunensis* Portenko	Asiatic or Central Asian Cuckoo	Iran, south USSR Himalayas	Smaller and paler, especially immature [than nominate race]
Cuculus canorus telephonus Heine	Japanese Cuckoo	Japan	Underparts barred finer and less black

3 | Migration

Common Cuckoos migrate between a vast European and Asian breeding range and an equally extensive wintering range in sub-Saharan
Africa and tropical Asia. A similar migration is achieved by millions of
birds of many families, ranging in size from tiny warblers to the larger
birds of prey and storks. A high proportion are insectivorous birds
unable to survive a northern hemisphere winter, the Cuckoo and the
Honey Buzzard, *Pernis apivorus*, representing two of the largest and more
specialized insect feeders to undertake this long journey twice a year.
Centuries ago the usual view was that Swallows, *Hirundo rustica*, for
example, hibernated in the mud of ponds and that the Cuckoo turned
into a Sparrowhawk in winter, beliefs dating back at least to the days of
Aristotle and Pliny.

A total absence in the northern hemisphere, together with numerous
sightings of migrating birds in Africa and Europe, plus the frequent
sighting and collection of birds in Africa in winter, form the bulk of
evidence for migration by Cuckoos. This is supported by the recovery in
Africa south of the Sahara of only two birds ringed in Europe.

Even less information is available on the movements of Cuckoos
occupying the eastern part of the breeding range. Many birds probably
move south from northern Asia to winter in southern India and the
tropical south-east Asia islands as far as New Guinea. Some, however,
also migrate to Africa, as do Lesser Cuckoos which breed in eastern Asia.
The following description of migration in Common Cuckoos is confined
to the birds from the western half of the breeding range.

Departure from Africa

The distribution of Cuckoos in Africa is confused by the presence of the
breeding African species *Cuculus gularis*, and two subspecies, *subtelephonus* from Asia and *bangsi* from Iberia, all of which are virtually
indistinguishable from one another in the field. It may be suspected
that Palaearctic Cuckoos move around following the rains and

consequent outbreaks of caterpillars, as do other resident cuckoos within Africa.

The only ring recoveries of European birds are from West Africa: a Dutch bird recovered in October in Togo, and a British bird found in January in the Cameroons. Perhaps the October bird was still on migration at the time. Many birds collected in West Africa have been assigned to the smaller *bangsi* race, and it seems likely that the nominate race had been largely overlooked there. With only two recoveries of ringed birds south of the Sahara, the migration of Cuckoos can only be pieced together from dates of specimens collected on expeditions and from observations by the comparatively few ornithologists to have worked in relevant areas.

In the west, occasional records exist from July to April with more birds noted on passage in autumn than in spring. There is evidence for Cuckoos migrating northward in Nigeria during March and April, and through Tangier mainly during the second half of April (Payn 1938; Smith 1968). The Iberian *bangsi* race may be entirely limited to West Africa.

In southern and eastern Africa, the spring passage is much more marked. Sightings of migratory Cuckoos are common in northern Zaire, Kenya, Uganda, and especially Tanzania. Quoting Sir Fred Jackson, Bannermann (1955) suggested that most Cuckoos in Africa travel through the Rift and Nile valleys in spring to converge on Egypt, from whence they cross the eastern Mediterranean using the islands, southern Greece, Sicily and Italy before invading north-west Europe. Some birds, he thought, may move westward along the south Mediterranean shore as far as Cyrenaica in Libya before crossing the sea.

More recently, Moreau (1972) considered that Cuckoos take off from near the equator, making a continuous flight of over 3,000km across the northern tropics and Sahara to arrive in North Africa in March and April. This involves a journey of about three days non-stop flight, a feat once thought impossible, but now known to be achieved by many small passerines. In order to undertake such journeys the birds accumulate large amounts of fuel in the form of fat, since there is little hope of refuelling en route in the North African desert. Despite rather more records of spring birds in Egypt than elsewhere, it seems likely that the migration is on a broad front covering the entire Mediterranean. Birds in north-east Africa may be destined for eastern Europe and the Soviet Union, a considerably larger area, with a potentially higher Cuckoo population than western Europe.

Arrival in Europe

The arrival of the first Cuckoos in Europe begins in March in the south, lasting until late May for the most northerly extremes of the breeding range. The return of Cuckoos as shown by records of first song has long aroused public interest and has been well-documented in many parts of Europe. De Smet (1967) claimed that dates of first songs were unsatisfactory for three reasons: there may be a time-lag between arrival and first call, the first call may be just an isolated individual, and recorders tend not to operate every day. He instanced three cases where birds were seen before they were heard, giving a time-lag of 8 days in the Netherlands, 11 days in Belgium and 12 in France. Molnar (1944) also recorded Cuckoos in Hungary about 10 days before hearing the first song. Migrating Cuckoos, however, are notoriously silent and it seems likely that sighted non-singing individuals are birds on passage to more northerly latitudes. At my study site in Cambridgeshire in 1975, two Cuckoos called briefly in the early morning of 19 April, but the first strongly-singing male did not appear until 24 April. As no Cuckoos were heard or seen during the intervening four days, the earlier birds were thought to be on passage. Other observers in breeding habitats apparently have not seen birds before hearing the first song, and I think that it is reasonable to assume that Cuckoos sing within a day or two of arrival at their breeding sites. Adverse weather or food shortage however, may greatly reduce song output.

Despite his objections to first song records, De Smet (1970) collected data from all over Europe between 1961 and 1965, and plotted the results in groups of 3 or 4 degrees of latitude in periods of seven days. He found that, in general, Cuckoos advanced northwards at about half a degree of latitude (55km) per day. From latitude 40°N in central Spain, southern Italy, Greece and Turkey to latitude 70°N in northern Scandinavia, Cuckoos arrived from the end of March to the end of May respectively, a period of two months.

A similar study in Germany between 1948 and 1957 (Brüns and Nocke 1959) showed that the average arrival date in the south of that country was 18 April, in the centre 23 April, and in the north, 29 April. These dates agree with those of De Smet, although they stem from different sources and different years. In eastern France, Claudon (1955) gave extreme dates of first songs between 1946 and 1955 as 7–15 April (average 11 April), which again fits De Smet's results.

The timing of migration into the breeding range is probably associated with the food availability, with most birds arriving only when their survival is assured. De Smet (1970) considered that woodland habitats were occupied before any other and Claudon (1955) noted that lowland regions were occupied 8–12 days earlier than altitudes above 182m. No geographic features appear to present barriers to migrating Cuckoos, as birds cross the Mediterranean possibly even at its widest; also the Pyrenees and Alps, the English Channel and the North Sea. Climatic conditions in different years and in different regions similarly do not apparently affect spring arrival, the earliest birds arriving in the north before the last snow and ice of winter has melted and prior to the appearance of leaves on the trees.

Arrival in Great Britain

As in northern Africa and southern Europe, Cuckoos arrive along the entire southern coast of England though, of course, not all necessarily stop there on route to their breeding sites. *The Handbook of British Birds* (Witherby *et al.* 1938) gives the main arrival date as the second week of April, but Bannerman (1955) and others consider that the third week of April forms the average date. According to the data collected by De Smet (1970) the main arrival in Great Britain occurs between 17 and 23 April in the south, 24–30 April in the north, and 1–7 May in the extreme north and Scottish islands. These dates are based on records of first singing males heard. Naturally there is a spread of males arriving probably over several weeks.

Table 7 gives an indication of the average arrival in Britain from a variety of sources dating from 1736. The combined results for southern England (as far north as Northamptonshire/Norfolk) show that 18 April is the average arrival date for first Cuckoos. In northern Britain early birds appear on average in the last week in April.

Cuckoos have been recorded in Britain in all months but the very few winter records are open to suspicion. A bird was reportedly seen and heard singing in Surrey on 20 February 1953 (Buchan-Hepburn 1955) which may have been a genuine early migrant, and another was re-corded in Pembroke on 22 December 1954 (Roch and Roberts 1955). It was about this time that the Collared Dove, *Streptopelia decaocto*, began to colonize Britain and there is now common confusion between this dove and the Cuckoo.

Mode of migration

Males are thought to arrive before females, although the evidence for this is slight. Females are not conspicuous before the laying season starts and could be easily missed. Some authors have suggested that males

Table 7   *Arrival of Cuckoos in Great Britain from records of first call*
(*data mainly from Bannerman 1955 and local bird reports*)

Region	Years	Number of years	Earliest	Latest	Average
Isle of Wight	–	–	11.4	15.4	13.4
Dungeness Bird Observatory	1957–1968	12	1.4	27.4	18.4
Kent	–	–	–	–	13.4
Sussex	–	–	11.4	18.4	14.4
Lundy Island	1965–1973	9	20.3	28.4	16.4
Blaxhall, Suffolk		20	9.4	–	22.4
Lowestoft, Suffolk	1910–1927	18	–	–	22.4
Bedfordshire	1946–1972	27	–	–	16.4
Huntingdonshire	1949–1970	22	9.4	22.4	14.4
Cambridgeshire	1921–1973	53	3.4	24.4	15.4
Oundle, Northamptonshire	1938–1973	36	11.4	3.5	23.4
Northamptonshire	1884–1969	86	24.3	30.4	16.4
Norfolk (Marsham records)	1736–1925	189	12.4	7.5	25.4
Norfolk (Whitear 1884)	1809–1826	18	17.4	3.5	25.4
Norfolk Bird Reports	1954–1972	19	29.3	26.4	15.4
Lincolnshire	1911–1972	62	16.4	25.5	26.4
North Devon (Palmer 1946)	–	–	–	–	22.4
Thames Valley	1958–1965	8	28.3	10.4	5.4
Snowdonia (Condry 1966)	–	–	–	–	21.4
Lancashire	–	–	–	–	29.4–8.5
Calf of Man	1967–1972	6	22.4	30.4	25.4
County Mayo (Ruttledge 1921)	1914–1920	7	20.4	27.4	25.4
Bradford, Yorkshire	1879–1906	14	12.4	4.5	22.4

precede their mates by as much as three weeks, others estimate one week or a few days. Still others (e.g. Chance 1940) have maintained that where a territory was already established, a pair may arrive and even migrate together. Presumably, however, there is an overlap in arrival times, with males, on average, earlier. Results at my Cambridgeshire study (Table 8) show that males were recorded earlier than females by about seven days on average over six years.

Table 8   *Arrival of male and female Cuckoos at Cambridgeshire study site 1974–1979*

Year	Record of: First male	First female	Days apart
1974	28.4	4.5	6
1975	19.4	2.5	13
1976	4.5	21.5	17
1977	28.4	29.4	1
1978	1.5	4.5	3
1979	6.5	11.5	5
		MEAN = 7.5 days	

As in many migrant species, Cuckoos tend to return annually to the same breeding site. The record for a female is held by one studied by Blaise (1965) in France which returned for 8 years. There are records of individual males with peculiarities in their songs returning annually to the same places for 8 years (Gurney 1899), 10 years in County Down (Burton 1900), 10 years in Berkshire (van de Weyer 1928), and 9 years in Lancashire (Dooly 1928).

The Cuckoo is generally assumed to be a nocturnal migrant, although again the evidence is slight. Cuckoos have been recorded at lighthouses at night during autumn migration: at Bardsey Island, Wales (Evans 1969) and at Hiddensee, Germany (Nisbet 1957). Observations of daytime migration are quite numerous, indicating that some progress is made during the day, and for birds travelling over large stretches such as the Mediterranean or Sahara, migration must continue day and night. In southern Europe and Africa, Cuckoos have occasionally been seen in large numbers, apparently on passage during the day. Such movement might be slow as birds fly from tree to tree feeding on caterpillars. Rappe (1965) presented numerous records of diurnal migration in Cuckoos.

Cuckoos are normally solitary birds and tend to migrate singly or in very small groups. Clay and Meinertzhagen (1933) reported a 'spectacular passage' on 21 April through Port Gavarnie in the Pyrenees, and 'large numbers' were reported through Tangiers during April (Payn 1938). Incoming birds often congregate on small islands. Sharrock (1973) recorded up to 14 birds together on Cape Clear Island in spring, and Meinertzhagen (1948) counted up to 80 on 3 May on Ushant Island, Brittany. There are several records of groups of up to 50 Cuckoos in various parts of Britain in spring and late summer, suggesting that some birds travel together (see *Brit. Birds* 1980, 73: 412–414). Most records of migrating Cuckoos, however, refer to single birds, and at one breeding site it would be unusual for all the inhabitants to arrive or depart at the same time.

Calling while on migration is unusual, although Moreau (1972) saw many birds between 30 March and 2 April in Tanzania 'chasing each other and uttering excited bubbling calls'. At this time they were presumably migrating north.

From European ringing results, Seel (1977b) estimated the speed of movement of Cuckoos on their southward migration by two methods, arriving at figures of about 20km per day for young birds and in a range 20–70km per day for all age groups combined. His methods were based on (i) the general appearance of ringed birds in north and south Europe, and (ii) direct ring recoveries of birds recaptured during the same autumn. These compare with De Smet's figure of 55km per day based on earliest songs through Europe in spring. The great variability in speed of migration as shown by ringing results was interpreted by Seel as evidence that Cuckoos make frequent stops to feed while migrating south. This may be especially important in birds of the year, since in Britain, at least, they have a lower body weight than adults (Seel 1977a).

Speeds of Cuckoos in ordinary flight have been measured as 27mph (Spector 1956) and in a range 23–27mph (Meinertzhagen 1955). Taking an average normal flying speed of 25mph (40km per hour), in a non-stop flight of 12 hours, a Cuckoo might travel 480km, roughly the length of England. On migration a Cuckoo is likely to travel at higher speeds than 40km per hour, and to take advantage of prevailing winds.

Autumn migration

Compared with other summer visitors to the Palaearctic, Cuckoos leave their breeding sites notoriously early. In some cases suitable host nests are still available until the end of July, or even mid-August in Reed Warblers, yet most adult Cuckoos leave during July. Lack of parental responsibilities may permit early departure, but this does not account for departure during a potential breeding season. Lack (1968) suggested that cessation of egg-laying and subsequent departure may be primarily determined by the food supply: the Cuckoo's main food, caterpillars, may become less abundant in July. On the other hand, independent young Cuckoos, the diets of which are known to include at least some hairy caterpillars, survive in the breeding range for a month or more after the adults have gone. Either young birds exploit a mainly different food supply, or find enough typical Cuckoo food in July and August to allow, not only growth and survival, but some pre-migratory fattening. A more detailed study of the food of adults and independent young is clearly needed to elucidate the reason for this seemingly premature departure. Young of the North American cuckoos apparently migrate south at the same time as their parents in August and September, when grasshoppers are important in the diet (Beal 1898). It is possible that European Cuckoos also feed on grasshoppers in Europe before migrating to Africa. This would provide them with a fat-rich food source, ideal for rapid fuel deposition.

Departure from Britain

Towards the end of June male Cuckoos stop singing in their British breeding areas and apparently leave. Females that have finished laying also probably go by the end of June. Other females may be seen up to two or three weeks after the last male is heard. At my study site, females were still laying eggs after males had stopped singing in most years. Table 9 shows that females were recorded later than males by 0–17 days, about 6 days later on average. This compares with males preceding females in spring by a similar time period. Of course, with reduced song output towards the end of the breeding season, males may still be present but unnoticed. Similarly, females could become more secretive in the absence of males, so they too could easily be overlooked and be present longer than recorded. As with arrival, there is presumably an overlap of the sexes during departure.

Table 9 also shows that the apparent disappearance of males, excluding the unusual 1976 season, preceded the end of egg-laying by 1–8 days, or about 3 days on average. Owen (1933), studying Cuckoos in

Table 9   *Departure of male and female Cuckoos at Cambridgeshire study site 1973–1979*

Year	Record of: Last male	Last female	Days apart	Date last egg
1973	–	8.7	–	7.7
1974	10.7	14.7	4	11.7
1975	30.6	9.7	9	8.7
1976	28.6	28.6	0	9.6
1977	28.6	15.7	17	29.6
1978	11.7	16.7	5	14.7
1979	7.7	10.7	3	10.7
			MEAN = 6.3 days	

Kent in 1912–1933 recorded the last male song there on 9 July, and also remarked that freshly laid eggs could be found 3–4 days after cessation of male song. It would seem unlikely, perhaps, that females vacate their laying ranges immediately after laying the last egg, but they may remain for only a few more days. True migration may not occur until after a period of local dispersal from breeding sites; most British Cuckoos move in a general south-easterly direction to reach continental Europe (Seel 1977b).

Contrary to early songs, few people keep records of when Cuckoos are last heard. The scanty data available on late adults in Britain suggest that they are not normally present later than August. Most have left by the end of July, with migration extending from late June until about the third week in August.

Young Cuckoos ringed in the British Isles are mainly recovered to the south-east in continental Europe (Seel 1977b). It seems they travel relatively short distances during the initial stages of migration, following a period of general dispersal from the natal area in almost any direction. It has been suggested that such dispersal could assist in 'imprinting' to the natal site. I have found, however, that young Cuckoos, like adults, disappear from the breeding site rather abruptly. Many probably die, but two which were marked and came back in the next year had left the breeding site only 15 and 16 days after fledging, although both were fed by their respective foster parents on the last day they were seen. These two birds apparently dispersed from the breeding site immediately on reaching independence, yet returned to it in later years.

Early young Cuckoos could begin their autumn migration at the same time as adults, although their lower body weight might necessitate more frequent stops to feed. The exodus of young British Cuckoos occurs in August, about one month later than adults. Young birds may still be seen in Britain into September, rarely into October or November. Very late birds could be on passage from more northerly latitudes, or late-hatched offspring – e.g. a young Cuckoo still dependent on hosts on 17 October (King 1937), or birds which have 'gone wrong'. The majority have left by the end of August, most travelling south or south-east.

Departure from Europe

Documented records of late male songs in continental Europe are rare. Ringing recoveries show that some adult Cuckoos may be found throughout Europe in August and September with about equal numbers of recoveries north and south of latitude 48°N (Seel 1977b). Main arrivals of adults in Egypt, Sinai and Palestine occurs during the second half of August and into September (Verheyen 1951). Early birds have been reported from 8 July (Palestine) and in the second half of July (Egypt). The majority of adults have left Europe by the end of August. Apparently Cuckoos have not been recorded in southern Europe feeding up in preparation for the journey across the Mediterranean and Sahara.

Young Cuckoos ringed in western continental Europe show a slightly different orientation to British-ringed nestlings (Seel 1977b). Whereas British birds move mainly south-east, the larger movements (over 200km) of continental youngsters are mainly south or south-west. Seel interpreted this as a possible population distinction between British and continental Cuckoos but the evidence for this is slight. Similarly, Verheyen's (1951) suggestion of three distinct European populations on the basis of migration directions seems groundless.

Cuckoo migration through Europe, therefore, extends from late June to October, with adults leaving first followed by the young, and on a broad front probably stopping in southern Europe before crossing into Africa. Bannerman (1955) thought that most north-west European Cuckoos crossed the Mediterranean on the eastern side, since autumn birds were mainly recorded in Egypt and the Near East countries. But Moreau (1972) suggested that non-stop flights of over 3,000km were likely in autumn as well as spring, taking Cuckoos directly from southern Europe to equatorial Africa.

A possible exception to this could be the Iberian *bangsi* race, which may migrate south through Spain crossing the western Mediterranean into northern and western Africa, and thence to tropical West Africa.

Arrival in Africa

Although autumn Cuckoos are first noted in July in north-east Africa, fewer birds are recorded there in autumn than in spring. Autumn migration through Ethiopia occurs from mid-August until the end of September, and through Chad between 30 August and 6 September (Salvan 1967–9). Early birds are reported from Uganda on 29 July and north-east Tanzania on 26 July, but main arrival in equatorial countries occurs from the end of August until mid-November, reaching countries south of the equator mainly in November and December.

In the west, autumn Cuckoos pass through Senegal from mid-August to mid-October, reaching Togo and Nigeria chiefly in November and December, and possibly moving further east and south during December and January.

Cuckoos are not noted in numbers north of the equator in Africa in spring, which is the end of the dry season there. But in autumn, the steppe country to the south of the Sahara is green at the end of the rains, with a good supply of insect food. In southern Africa the climatic conditions are reversed, with the rainy season extending from October/November until April when most migrants have left or are leaving (Moreau 1966). Cuckoos from Europe, therefore, may not have to travel as far as they do in spring in order to find food on migration. This might help to explain why adult Cuckoos migrate so early: it could be beneficial for them to reach the southern Sahara in time to exploit an abundant caterpillar supply there at the end of the rains. As the food supply dwindles with the onset of the dry season, Cuckoos pass south of the equator to arrive in southern Africa in November when the rains there should be providing ample food. The southern rains end in April by which time Cuckoos are already well north. African cuckoo species which breed in the extreme south apparently leave in late December or early January, so perhaps the food supply diminishes then, and all cuckoos relying on caterpillars or grasshoppers move northward in January and February. The main migration of European Cuckoos to the Palaearctic would then begin in March.

4 | Food

Cuckoos are mainly insectivorous birds renowned for favouring hairy, warningly-coloured and sometimes toxic caterpillars which few other birds eat. They have thus specialized on a diet which is largely unexploited by other animals. A universal predilection for caterpillars is common to almost all species of cuckoos regardless of whether they are parasitic or not. We can assume, therefore, that the development of this diet occurred prior to the evolution of brood parasitism within the family. Indeed, it would have been very convenient if such a unique diet was the prerogative of only the parasitic species, since the two habits could have been more positively linked. It would be easy to imagine that hairy caterpillars might be unsuitable for rearing young. This is not the case, however, because non-parasitic cuckoos successfully rear their young on such food. Nevertheless, few dietary studies of parasitic or nesting cuckoos have been made and it seems a logical step to compare the feeding habits of the two groups in more detail.

Prey items

Most of the information on the food of cuckoos stems from a rather haphazard examination of specimens and from casual field observations. The relative importance of particular prey types is not easily assessed as cuckoos are difficult birds to collect in any numbers, and observations of feeding individuals tend to be accidental. A cuckoo can rarely be watched for long periods to determine its feeding rate or to identify particular food items.

The usual foods identified for the European Cuckoo (Table 10) are caterpillars, mainly those of butterflies and moths (lepidoptera). These may be of almost any kind but are often hairy, colonial and brightly-marked. Notable early in the Cuckoo's breeding season in Britain are those of the Drinker moth which grow to about 80mm and occur commonly on grasses and sedges in a wide variety of open and marshy habitats. Cuckoos have been observed to devour large numbers of these

Table 10 *List of prey species of British Cuckoos*
(compiled from Collinge 1925, Witherby, et al. 1938, and additional sources in literature)

Lepidoptera larvae	
Small Tortoiseshell butterfly, *Aglais urticae*	S,T,G
Peacock butterfly, *Nymphalis io*	S,T,G
Large White butterfly, *Pieris brassicae*	W,D,G,A
Small White butterfly, *Pieris rapae*	
Hawk moths, *Sphingidae* spp.	C,W
Buff-tip moth, *Phalera bucephala*	H,W,G
Antler moth, *Cerapteryx graminis*	A
Gold-tail moth, *Euproctis similis*	H,W
Lackey moth, *Malacosoma neustria*	H,W,T,G
Oak Eggar moth, *Lasiocampa quercus*	H
Drinker moth, *Philudoria potatoria*	H,W
Lappet moth, *Gastropacha quercifolia*	H,C
Small Eggar moth, *Eriogaster lanestris*	H,W,T,G
Figure of eight moth, *Diloba caeruleocephala*	H,W
Ermine moths, *Spilosoma* spp.	H
Garden Tiger moth, *Arctia caja*	H
Cinnabar moth, *Callimorpha jacobaeae*	W,D,G
March moth, *Alsophila aescularia*	C
Winter moth, *Operophtera brumata*	A
Early Thorn moth, *Selenia bilunaria*	C
Magpie moth, *Abraxas grossulariata*	W
Mottled Umber moth, *Erannis defoliaria*	A
Dotted Border moth, *Erannis marginaria*	C,A
Six-spot Burnet moth, *Zygaena filipendulae*	D
Green Oak-roller moth, *Tortrix viridana*	A

Coleoptera adult beetles and their larvae (mostly unidentified)

Click beetle, *Corymbites cupreus*
Hymenoptera, sawflies and their larvae

Gooseberry sawfly, *Nematus ribesii*
Pine sawfly, *Diprion pini*

Diptera flies and their larvae
Crane fly, *Tipula paludosa*
Hoverflies, *Syrphidae* spp.

Odonata unidentified dragonflies, especially damselflies, *Zygoptera*
Dermaptera, earwigs

Also (mainly unidentified): centipedes, spiders, ants, worms, slugs, snails, bird eggs and nestlings.
Rarely: vegetable matter such as buds, seeds and berries

Key to letters: S = Spiny; H = Hairy; C = Cryptically-coloured; W = Warningly-coloured; D = Distasteful; T = Tent-living; G = Gregarious; A = Sporadically super-abundant.

14 A Reed Warbler feeding a fly to a 12-day-old young Cuckoo. The hosts bring a wide range of insect foods to their young, from tiny aphids to large butterflies and damselflies

15 Typical food of adult Cuckoos – hairy gregarious caterpillars of the buff-tip moth

16 Another common Cuckoo food item is the hairy and warningly-coloured caterpillar of the gold-tail moth commonly found on hawthorn hedges in June. *Photo: N. J. Westwood*

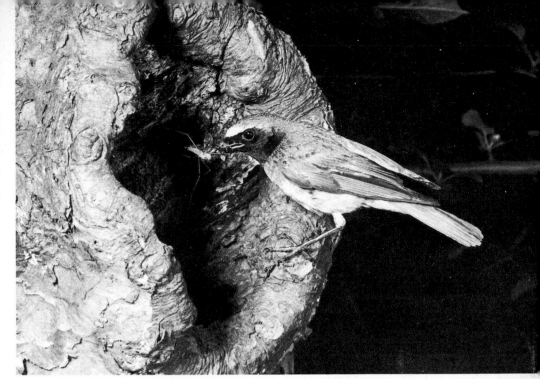

17 and **18** Two common hosts of the Cuckoo, both of which lay blue eggs. Cuckoos victimizing Redstarts, *Phoenicurus phoenicurus* (above), in Scandinavia and Continental Europe lay blue eggs mimicking the host's eggs, whereas Cuckoos victimizing Dunnocks, *Prunella modularis*, (below) in Britain, lay ill-matched eggs.
Photos: Eric Hosking

19 and **20** A female Cuckoo approaches a Reed Warbler's nest through the reeds. Note the use of the wings and tail for balancing, and the zygodactyl feet for clinging to the reeds

21 On arrival at the nest, the female Cuckoo picks up and holds one of the warbler's eggs in her bill while laying her own egg in its place. Sightings of Cuckoos flying around with eggs in their bills led to the earlier popular belief that the Cuckoo's own egg was carried to the nest in this way

22 A Cuckoo's egg is usually only slightly larger than the eggs of its hosts. Here the difference is easy to detect in a Reed Warbler's clutch

23 The young Cuckoo hatches in 11–12 days, usually in advance of the host's eggs

24 and **25** One by one the young Cuckoo ejects the eggs of the Reed Warbler by carrying them on its back up the side of the nest until they roll out. This incredible behaviour was first documented by Edward Jenner in 1788

caterpillars in spring. Condry (1966), for example, saw one bird take 20 from only a few square metres of Snowdonian hillside, and in the fens of East Anglia it is not unusual to see dozens of Cuckoos, males and females alike, all in a small area taking Drinker moth caterpillars. Other important early caterpillars include those of the Garden Tiger, Lappet, Oak Eggar, Lackey, Yellow-tail, Winter moth and several others. Most of these hibernate as larvae during the winter and emerge in spring to feed and grow before pupating. Their availability, therefore, depends on winter survival and upon the stimulus of increasing temperatures in the spring. Once they become active it may be still some time before they reach a size suitable for Cuckoos. In late springs few, if any, of these caterpillars are available, but alternative Cuckoo foods are largely unknown. Possibly the birds rely more on terrestrial beetles and spiders at such times. Observations in Monks Wood National Nature Reserve in the cold spring of 1978 revealed that all the Cuckoos (some 15 or more) were obtaining their food from the forest floor, mainly in rides and clearings, and the droppings of those captured contained many beetle elytra and a few larval mouthparts. Although fairly abundant in April and May, beetles remain relatively inconspicuous and are only active (and therefore presence-revealing) on warm, sunny days. Not surprisingly in cold springs Cuckoos seem rather scarce, inactive and silent, presumably because they have to spend more time searching for food which is small and widely distributed in the environment.

Analyses of European Cuckoo stomachs confirm that caterpillars and beetles form the bulk of their prey. Collinge (1925) looked at 20 stomachs and reported that lepidoptera larvae and beetles comprised 58.5 per cent and 14.5 per cent respectively of the total diet. Lowe (1943) found that the stomachs he examined invariably contained a closely packed mass of caterpillars or beetles and for 4 Scottish specimens examined in more detail, one contained entirely click beetles, the others held caterpillars of the Winter moth and Mottled Umber moth. In Russia, 19 specimens also contained mainly caterpillars and beetles (Dement'ev et al. 1966). In an analysis of 82 stomachs of the Japanese Common Cuckoo Cuculus canorus telephonus, Ishizawa and Chiba (1966) found lepidoptera larvae constituted about 75 per cent of the food taken whereas other insects, including ants and beetles, comprised about 20 per cent.

As temperatures increase in spring and caterpillars become active and larger, Cuckoos consume them in increasing quantities, until by the end of May the diet consists almost entirely of caterpillars such as those mentioned. Another favoured prey at this time is the larvae of the Magpie moth which are warningly-coloured and distasteful, and occur on a wide range of food plants in a great many habitats. Bottomley and Bottomley (1975) photographed up to 4 male Cuckoos feeding together on Magpie moth caterpillars in late May in Cornwall, while Armitage (1978) recorded one feeding on these in early June in Yorkshire. In June Cuckoos may be seen systematically searching along hedges for the hairy red, white and black caterpillars of the Gold-tail moth. I once collected about 200 of these larvae and placed them on an isolated bush in a Cuckoo breeding area. Within a few hours two Cuckoos had located and eaten them all. Towards the end of the Cuckoo's breeding season (late June–early July), the colonial larvae of the Small Tortoiseshell and Peacock butterflies on nettlebeds become common prey items. These may also be available to early-fledging young which later consume Cinnabar moth caterpillars commonly found on ragwort. Crawshaw (1963) watched an independent young Cuckoo picking up and eating these caterpillars during the last week of July in Essex, and in their film, *The Petersfinger Cuckoos*, E. and T. Channel confirmed this behaviour with some excellent photography.

In the winter range it seems that hairy caterpillars are again the usual prey, along with termites and grasshoppers. Species of African cuckoos depend largely on hairy caterpillars and it is likely that migrant Palae-arctic Cuckoos feed on similar prey species, and make seasonal movements within Africa following the rains and associated food. African parasitic cuckoos apparently consume a wide range of caterpillars, but orthoptera (grasshoppers, crickets and locusts) are also regular in the diet.

Parasitic cuckoos elsewhere in the world are well-known specialists on hairy caterpillars, but they consume many other insects as well. The main exceptions are the Koel, *Eudynamis scolopaceae*, and the Channel-billed Cuckoo, *Scythrops novaehollandiae*. Both these species eat mainly fruit including even poisonous ones such as the fruits of the Yellow Oleander. They thus have a diet in common with many other fruit-eating birds and animals but, like their insectivorous cuckoo relatives, they have the ability to cope with toxic foods. They also feed on hairy caterpillars, bugs, various other insects, snails, and even flower nectar (Ali and Ripley 1969). Other cuckoos also take fruits at times but these rarely reach significant proportions in any one species' diet.

In as much as parasitic cuckoos specialize on caterpillars as their main source of food, it is noticeable that they concentrate on the more conspicuous types rather than cryptic, sparsely distributed or small, unobtrusive ones. Similarly, other insect foods are often distasteful or foul-smelling and otherwise rejected by insectivorous animals. Conspicuous or gregarious insects of almost any kind are the preferred prey.

The diets of non-parasitic cuckoos also include caterpillars and other large insects, and it is difficult to see any major differences between the foods taken by these and their parasitic relatives. Several non-parasitic species have been observed to feed their young on hairy, spiny or toxic caterpillars with no apparent ill-effects. Skutch (1966), for example, saw a Squirrel Cuckoo, *Piaya cayana*, in tropical America feeding its young on a large spiny caterpillar which he described as extremely venomous and likely to cause excruciating pain to human skin. Some Neotropical cuckoos, notably the lizard cuckoos, *Saurothera* spp., specialize on reptiles, and the Roadrunner, *Geococcyx californianus*, feeds its young mainly on Whip-tailed lizards (Ohmart 1973). Adult Road-runners, however, eat mainly insects, although they reportedly kill and devour venomous rattlesnakes. In the same region, anis (Crotophagi-nae) feed on insects which they hunt by following grazing animals or even by following columns of army ants which flush larger insects in their path. According to Skutch (1959) Groove-billed Anis, *C. sulcirostris*, usually bring grasshoppers to their young. Old World coucals (Centro-podinae) feed on a variety of small reptiles, amphibians and small birds, but insects, especially caterpillars and grasshoppers, probably form the bulk of their food.

The best-studied diets of non-parasitic cuckoos are those of two North American species, the Yellow- and Black-billed Cuckoos, *Coccyzus americanus* and *C. erythropthalmus*. These species are particularly associ-ated with outbreaks of tent-building caterpillars which few other birds will touch. In some years such caterpillars are super-abundant in May and June when the cuckoos return from their tropical winter range in South America. Concentrations of the birds occur wherever there are local outbreaks of caterpillars. In an analysis of 155 stomachs of these two species Beal (1898) found that caterpillars comprised nearly half the yearly food (May–October), but perhaps his most significant discovery was that in July and August, the main breeding period, caterpillars were not as frequent prey as grasshoppers. In May caterpillars represented 60 per cent of the diet and grasshoppers only 3 per cent, while in July the proportion of grasshoppers had risen to 43 per cent. Other observers have recorded orthoptera as frequent food items brought to young *Coccyzus* cuckoos. While tent caterpillars are clearly important food for these cuckoos on arrival in spring and possibly during egg-production, they have pupated by the time the young cuckoos hatch, and then orthoptera, as well as other hairy caterpillars, have become more abun-dant. Nolan and Thompson (1975) have suggested that annual and periodic cicadas may be the largest readily caught insects available during the main breeding period, but Beal (1898) found that they represented only about about 6.5 per cent of the yearly food. Other items recorded as occasional prey of these cuckoos include beetles, flies, butterflies, dragonflies, ants, sawfly larvae, spiders, small frogs, lizards and small fruits. The diet would appear to be not significantly different from that found in parasitic cuckoos, except that grasshoppers may be more important food for young non-parasitic species.

It remains to be investigated whether such an apparently small difference is of any significance in terms of the evolution of brood parasitism in the family. If grasshoppers, not caterpillars, were the principal food for rearing young non-parasitic cuckoos, the inference is that a species which could not find these insects in sufficient quantity might become parasitic. Instead of nesting late in the year (like North American Cuckoos) to exploit a grasshopper supply suitable for rearing young, the parasite could lay its eggs earlier to coincide with the abundance of caterpillars as well as the nesting period of most of the likely host species.

Feeding strategy

Cuckoos are solitary feeders which very occasionally form small groups to exploit a particularly abundant local food supply. Records of group feeding by European Cuckoos are quite rare suggesting that it is not common and that individuals normally range independently in search of food. Even a pair, if in fact Cuckoos form proper pair-bonds, probably do not feed together and only come in contact with one another at the breeding site. Hence the far-carrying and distinctive calls of the two sexes. Cuckoos are silent when feeding and perform no displays to advertise a locally abundant food source, so occasional group feeding is probably fortuitous. The fact that they do sometimes feed together, however, illustrates that they are not strictly territorial. In Woodwalton Fen, Cambridgeshire, I have seen up to 50 adult Cuckoos feeding in only about two hectares of marshy ground in May, and in nearby Monks Wood at least nine individually marked birds were seen to feed in one woodland ride about 200m in length. Field (1962) saw up to seven adults feeding on larvae of the Six-spot Burnet moth in June in Buckinghamshire. Sightings of two, three or four birds feeding together can be made at almost any time during the breeding season.

In his books (1922, 1940) Edgar Chance barely once mentioned the food or feeding behaviour of the birds under intensive observation for five years at his breeding site. Presumably he saw no feeding activity. Nor have other students of breeding Cuckoos recorded the feeding behaviour of their birds, and at my study site I have rarely seen birds feeding. I believe that most Cuckoos have more or less separate feeding and breeding ranges, although this could vary according to the distribution of the particular host species. One female I followed by radio telemetry in 1979 gathered nearly all her food in May and June at one site which was 3.2 and 2.6km away from two sites where she laid all her eggs. These two egg-laying places (the hosts were Reed Warblers) were 1.6km apart, and the bird visited both for long periods every day during the breeding season. The feeding site, an area of railway scrub with abundant caterpillars, was shared with at least three other females and about four males. Having non-exclusive feeding ranges explains why many birds may be found in a locally good feeding place such as Woodwalton Fen, and the distance from the food to the laying site explains why the birds are apparently absent from their breeding areas for several hours or a few days. Furthermore, the distance a Cuckoo has to travel between its breeding site and its food supply could be important for its breeding potential: the further it has to travel the more energy it will use in commuting rather than in egg-production. Being brood parasites, however, allows Cuckoos to travel great distances in search of suitable food. From a wide area containing many suitable breeding sites Cuckoos could converge on only a few reliable feeding places which they could not easily defend because of being away so much. Hostilities towards one another at such sites need not be great, since the birds are simply foraging, not defending a mate or breeding area.

The Cuckoo's main strategy when searching for food is to perch silent and motionless on a suitable vantage point from which it can scan the surrounding environment. It does not actively search for food but relies on keen eyesight and on the prey revealing itself by movement. Such a hunting method is only suited to the capture of quite large prey. The length of time spent watching from any one post depends upon the nature of the prey available. When the food is widely dispersed and relatively small, frequent changes of position are necessary, a bird rarely spending more than a few minutes in one place. Longer survey periods from the same perch are rewarding when there are large or gregarious caterpillars to be found.

Typical vantage points used when searching for food are exposed branches of trees, telegraph poles or wires, fence posts and bare rocks. A hunting Cuckoo perches upright, alert to any movement within a range of about 50m. The whole attitude resembles a hunting hawk. On sighting a suitable insect a Cuckoo glides swiftly to seize it, and may eat it on the spot or return to a feeding post where it can deal with the catch. When a colony of caterpillars is found a Cuckoo will scramble about rather clumsily gorging itself on the easily captured prey. An individual's stomach can contain vast numbers of caterpillars. K. G. Blaire, reported by Lowe (1943), counted 70 and 300 caterpillars in each of two specimens examined. For the similarly-sized American cuckoos Bent (1940) recorded 100 forest tent caterpillars in one stomach and Beal (1898) counted 217 in another. In this respect cuckoos are clearly opportunist feeders.

Other hunting methods may be employed according to the type of prey. Green (1928) wrote of a male Cuckoo 'trotting up and down' his lawn edge and pulling out worms and grubs. A bird feeding on Magpie moth caterpillars in a hedge was seen to perch on the ground below and periodically jump into the air to snatch individual larvae (Armitage 1978). Two London observers (Anon 1961) saw four Cuckoos systematically flapping furiously on the tops of young pine trees, then flying clumsily to the ground suggesting that they were dislodging food (possibly larvae of the pine sawfly, *Diprion pini*) from the foliage and retrieving it in the rough grass below. Tropical cuckoos are known to 'hawk' flying termites, and American cuckoos have been seen to catch adult Monarch and Swallowtail butterflies by similar means.

Cuckoos obtain their food at any level, from the tops of tall mature trees to the ground. However, they feed mostly on or near the ground or in fairly low herbage. Many of the caterpillars they seek, especially the large final instars, descend their foodplants and move along the ground to pupate elsewhere. These are readily sought by Cuckoos. Some larvae when about to pupate climb vertical tree trunks or walls where they are highly vulnerable. Cuckoos can cling on to such sites, presumably with the aid of their zygodactyl feet. In the middle of an urban estate J. L. F. Parslow (pers. comm.) saw a young Cuckoo repeatedly taking caterpillars of the Large White butterfly from the wall of his house during a week in August.

A large hairy caterpillar will normally be dealt with by a Cuckoo by firstly working it through the mandibles from one end to the other before giving it a violent shake to dispel the gut contents. The caterpillar is then swallowed whole. It has been suggested that mandibulating the prey in this way may remove most of the hairs or defensive secretions, but it seems likely that this is a simple softening process rendering a large caterpillar more manageable. Smaller hairy caterpillars are swallowed whole without preparation so it is not essential for the hairs to be removed. Osmaston (1916) watched at close range how a Red-winged Crested Cuckoo, *Clamator coromondus*, dealt with hairy caterpillars: each was passed through the bill several times until, with a sideways movement of one mandible over the other, the skin was cut at both ends. The caterpillar, reduced to a flattened tube, was violently flicked to dispel the contents and then swallowed. In all other species, parasitic or not, large caterpillars are shaken in this manner, whereas smaller prey is swallowed intact.

Once in the stomach the indigestible hairs from caterpillars become arranged around the lining, sometimes giving it a 'furred' appearance. The lining is rather thin-walled and is occasionally pierced by the hairs (Lowe 1943). The proventriculus, however, being exceptionally large and well developed, has walls which are twice as thick as those of the stomach, and it is possibly here where the toxic secretions are neutralized by enzymes secreted from special glands. Cuckoos excrete indigestible matter by regurgitating pellets, and they have an ability to shed periodically the weak stomach lining, a mechanism that has also been found in the Starling, *Sturnus vulgaris*.

Courtship feeding

Courtship feeding is a widespread phenomenon in birds and describes the provision of food to a female by the male. It used to be regarded as an activity purely associated with strengthening the pair-bond, but studies on several species have shown that the food given to the female is of real benefit during egg-production (e.g. Royama 1966). Courtship feeding in the European Cuckoo seems very rare and I have only one record: a personal observation of an individually marked bird (Table 11). This female appeared on an exposed telegraph wire overlooking a meadow on 28 June 1976, having not laid any eggs to my knowledge in that drought season. A male appeared on the wire nearby holding a 50mm caterpillar in his bill and calling in a typical bowed posture with wings drooped and tail fanned. The female flew the two metres to him and snatched the caterpillar in flight, landing on the wire again to devour the meal. The male proceeded to sing and display vigorously to her until another male arrived on the wire. Soon the female took off with the first male in pursuit, presumably hopeful of mating, while the second male flew off a minute later in the opposite direction. No Cuckoos were seen there again that year, and no further eggs were laid.

Within the cuckoo family, particularly in tropical species, courtship feeding is a regularly reported event. Lack (1968) proposed that supplementary feeding enables a female brood parasite to lay more eggs than would otherwise be possible, an advantage when egg-mortality is high because of host discrimination. Most courtship feeding instances refer to the members of one genus, *Chrysococcyx*, the small bronze or glossy cuckoos of Africa, Asia and Australasia (Table 11). Friedmann (1968) stated that males of the four species in Africa often feed females,

Table 11 *Some reported cases of courtship feeding in cuckoos*

Species	Description	Reference
Parasitic		
Didric Cuckoo	(i) 'Caterpillars' brought to a female 8 times in 15 minutes	Reed 1968
	(ii) 'Hairy caterpillars', *Acraea* spp given to a female or juvenile 10 times in 6 minutes	Maclaren 1952
	(iii) '40mm caterpillars' given to presumed adult in two bouts of 5-10 minutes	Maclaren 1952
	(iv) 'caterpillars'	Beven 1943
	(v) 'pupae'	Jackson 1938
Emerald Cuckoo	Hairy caterpillars during copulation	Haydock 1950
Klaas Cuckoo	'Insects' given to female at least 3 times	Winterbottom 1939
Shining Cuckoo	Communal displays and court-ship feeding	in Friedmann 1968
Jacobin Cuckoo	Hairy caterpillars during copulation	Godfrey 1939 Liversidge 1971
Black Cuckoo	Large hairy orange caterpillars	(Young 1946) in Friedmann 1948
Lesser Cuckoo	Simulated behaviour without food in winter range	in Friedmann 1956
Cuckoo	One personal observation in Cambridgeshire: male giving caterpillar of ?Peacock butterfly to female	
Non-parasitic		
Yellow-billed Cuckoo	'Large green worm' during copulation	in Bent 1940
Black-billed Cuckoo	Green larva brought on two occasions	Spencer 1943
Dwarf Cuckoo	(i) Large moth during copulation	Thomas 1978
	(ii) Caterpillars always in copulation, pair holding each end of prey	Ralph 1975
Dark-billed Cuckoo	as (ii) above	in Ralph 1975
Smooth-billed Ani	as (ii) above	in Ralph 1975
Squirrel Cuckoo	Green caterpillar during copulation	Skutch 1966
Roadrunner	Lizards during copulation	Whitson 1976
Black Coucal	In every case male fed female during copulation	Vernon 1971

and there are several reported cases for the New Zealand Shining Cuckoo, *C. lucidus*. It is of great interest that in this genus also there are numerous observations of adults (usually males) feeding their own post-fledged young which have been initially reared by hosts.

No quantitative data on the amount of food given to an individual female has been recorded, and indeed it would be very difficult to obtain. If it could be shown that a regularly fed female laid more eggs than one that was not fed, this might give some support for the 'increased egg-production' theory.

On the other hand, food offering by a male to a female often accompanies copulation, and in some bird species seems to be an essential part of mating. Most reported instances of copulation in tropical cuckoos have involved food-presentation. The male approaches the female with the food dangling from his bill, and with various display movements such as tail-flicking or head-bowing according to species. A receptive female permits mounting during which both birds hold each end of the prey. The male then dismounts, leaving the food with the female.

The type of food offered by cuckoos during courtship feeding does not seem to differ from their usual prey — hairy caterpillars. Non-parasitic species apparently use similar foods that they bring to their young. Perhaps the clearest example of this is shown in the Roadrunner as pointed out by Whitson (1976). Adults feed principally on insects but give vertebrates, especially lizards, to their young. During courtship feeding, which often follows an elaborate and extensive variety of displays, the female Roadrunner is offered again mainly lizards which both partners hold in their bills during copulation.

Feeding of young parasitic cuckoos

Nestling parasitic cuckoos are fed, of course, on whatever food each particular host species normally brings to its own young. Not surprisingly, as most cuckoos are insectivorous, so too are the majority of hosts. About 90 per cent of all recorded hosts of European Cuckoos (see Chapter 7) are insectivorous, and no species of the other 10 per cent is known to have successfully reared a young Cuckoo. Although some seed-eating birds initially bring insects to their young, they soon switch to providing seeds alone. So a young Cuckoo hatched in the nest of a Linnet, *Acanthis cannabina*, for example, may survive for only a week. Some tropical glossy cuckoos *Chrysococcyx*, however, regularly parasitize granivorous weaverbirds by which their young are successfully reared. The two most frequent hosts of the African Didric Cuckoo, *C. caprius*, are the Masked Weaver, *Ploceus velatus*, and the Red Bishop, *Euplectes orix*.

The former feeds its young exclusively on insects, whereas the latter regurgitates seeds from its crop (Friedmann 1968). Young Didrics, therefore, have a wide tolerance of food items and methods of feeding.

Remarkably, as mentioned in the previous section, several species of parasitic cuckoos occasionally feed fledglings or even nestlings of their own species, even though they are being reared by a host species. It is in the *Chrysococcyx* genus that this behaviour is most common (Table 12). The provision of insect food by adult cuckoos could be especially beneficial to their young which have been raised by granivorous host species, but there is no evidence to suggest that this is normal behaviour by cuckoos which victimize only those hosts. The habit is open to various interpretations and still requires critical study. Fledgling-feeding has never been reliably reported for the European Cuckoo and it has been recorded for only one member of its genus – the Australian Pallid Cuckoo, *Cuculus pallidus*. An interesting observation by Bell (1965), who was apparently mobbed by an adult European Cuckoo when he approached a youngster being fed by Meadow Pipits, raises the question of whether Cuckoos ever take an interest in their own offspring. This romantic possibility has long been suspected, but the near total lack of observations weighs heavily against it.

Insectivorous hosts of Cuckoos bring a potentially huge range of food to the young in their care and it has been suggested that a pair will bring more food to a young Cuckoo than to a full brood of its own. This remains unsubstantiated and seems unlikely since a young Cuckoo increases in weight at about the same rate as a host's brood, at least during the period when the host's young would normally occupy the nest. The young parasite is thought to have a voracious appetite which the host pair has to work many times harder to satisfy. On the other hand, during observations at two different Wren nests both Curtis (1969) and Wilde (1974) found that the female Wren was capable of rearing a young Cuckoo by herself. I have found that a single Reed Warbler (her mate presumably died) was unable to rear a young Cuckoo. Occasionally a young Cuckoo cannot eject its fellow nestlings because of the position of the nest, yet the hosts are still capable of rearing all the young present. Thus Gautier (1968) found a pair of Black Redstarts, *Phoenicurus ochruros*, rearing two young Cuckoos in one nest, and Burton (1947) records a young Cuckoo in a Robin's nest with four host young which all fledged (see Chapter 10). When rearing a Cuckoo the hosts normally have only one mouth to feed which perhaps explains why it is thought that they feed a young Cuckoo more assiduously than their own young.

Reed Warblers feed young Cuckoos on a great variety of insects

Table 12 *Some reported cases of parasitic cuckoos feeding young of their own species*

Species	Host	Description	Reference
Didric Cuckoo	–	(i) Adult male feeding young with 21 caterpillars in 15 minutes	Moreau 1944
	None present	(ii) Two adults (possibly pair) feeding caterpillars to maybe 3 young	Maclaren 1952
	–	(iii) Adults feeding newly-fledged young	Smith 1957
	None present	(iv) Adult male feeding caterpillars to young	R. E. Symons in Friedmann 1948
	–	(v) Adult making 12 visits to feed either mate or full-grown young	Holman in Friedmann 1948
Klaas Cuckoo	–	(i) Adult feeding and accompanying newly-fledged young	Moreau & Moreau 1939
	None present	(ii) Adult male feeding dysdercid bugs to two young	Baird 1945
Emerald Cuckoo	None present	(i) Adult male feeding hairy caterpillar to young	Millar 1943
	None present	(ii) Adult male feeding white hairy caterpillars to young on 20 visits	Worman 1930
Shining Cuckoo	Grey Warbler	(i) Adult feeding young	Hursthouse 1944
	Yellow-tailed Thornbill	(ii) Presumed female feeding nestling in presence of host pair	Howe 1905
Pallid Cuckoo	*Acanthiza* sp	Adult feeding young along with about 10 other 'hosts'	Cooper 1958
Great Spotted Cuckoo	Pied Crow	Adult twice fed young on caterpillar and flew off in company	Mundy and Cook 1977
Thick-billed Cuckoo	Black Helmet Shrike	Circumstantial evidence of pair carrying caterpillars near party of hosts with young cuckoo	(Townley 1936) in Friedmann 1948
Koel	–	Reported as feeding own young	in Friedmann 1968
Channel-billed Cuckoo	–	Reported as feeding own young	in Friedmann 1968
Fan-tailed Cuckoo	–	Reported as feeding own young	in Friedmann 1968
Jacobin Cuckoo	–	Reported as feeding own young	in Ali & Ripley 1969

ranging from tiny aphids to butterflies and moths. At first I thought that providing a young Cuckoo with a full grown butterfly was an example of hosts giving rather larger and different foods than they would give their own young, but Brown and Davies (1949) recorded adult lepidoptera, even the Peacock butterfly, as occasional food brought to young Reed Warblers by their parents.

Once it has fledged, a young Cuckoo will hide in a nearby bush or tree and demand food from any passing bird. Its persistent food-begging call can be heard from some distance and no doubt attracts birds other than its foster parents, many of which may be carrying food to their own nestlings. Owen (1912) reported one Wren of a pair feeding a young Cuckoo in a Dunnock nest more fequently than it fed its own young in a nearby nest. There are even records of small birds feeding an adult Cuckoo: possibly they had at some time reared a young Cuckoo and misinterpreted the red gape of the adult.

On reaching independence at about five weeks old, a young Cuckoo quickly chooses the diet for which its kind is celebrated. This is not learnt from its parents which have probably left the breeding site anyway, but is purely instinctive. It now has to fend for itself and migrate many thousands of kilometres across vast areas of inhospitable country where there is no food of any kind.

Host-nest predation

Cuckoos have long been accused of being nest-predators of their potential hosts and there is now sufficient evidence to show that this is true (Table 13). Although female cuckoos usually eat one or more of the host's eggs when parasitizing a nest, they also occasionally or regularly destroy nests by eating all the eggs or young. A nest may be robbed

Table 13 *Some reported cases of host-nest predation by parasitic cuckoos*

Species	Description	Reference
European Cuckoo	(i) Female flushed from Skylark nest in which one egg intact, the other broken and sucked.	
	(ii) H. L. Wilson shot Cuckoo with mash of eggshells in 'crop' from at least 7 eggs (2 of Robin; 5 of Dunnock or Song Thrush.	

Table 13   *continued*

Species	Description	Reference
	(iii) Adult Cuckoo took and swallowed 3 eggs from Meadow Pipit nest on 5 May 1952.	Hereford Orn. Club 1954
	(iv) Adult killing nestling Meadow Pipits.	Milburn 1915
	(v) Adult carrying away young Pied Wagtail from its nest. Repeatedly knocked nestling on branch but not seen if eaten.	Marchant 1972
	(vi) Destruction of 3 eggs in Dunnock nest.	Wright 1955
	(vii) Female predation of Reed Warbler nests: 9 incidents, including predation of young	Wyllie 1975
	(viii) Adult killing nestlings.	Headley and Jourdain 1919
Jacobin Cuckoo	(i) A collected female specimen with eggshell and developed embryo of host *Pycnonotus barbatus* in oesophagus.	Payne 1974
	(ii) Adult chased from 2 nests of *Euplectes orix* in which eggs broken and nests damaged.	E. Pike in Friedmann 1956
Didric Cuckoo	Female entered nest of Thick-billed Weaver, emerged with host egg and swallowed contents.	Calder 1951 in Friedmann 1956
Emerald Cuckoo	Adult entered nest-hole of Olive Barbet containing noisy nestlings but driven off by host pair	Holliday and Tait 1953 in Friedmann 1956
Klaas Cuckoo	'Females apparently predate nests'.	Jensen and Clinning 1975
Shining Bronze Cuckoo	Adult removed 1 egg of host and 1 of its own species from nest of Yellow-tailed Thornbill.	Chalk 1950
Koel	Female took and swallowed 4 eggs of Red-whiskered Bulbul – 5 November 1930	Ali 1931

during the laying period of the host, during incubation, or when there are small young. There are several interpretations that can be made of such behaviour.

Firstly, the most obvious one, is that they rob nests simply for the food. The activity is confined to the females in the breeding season, when the host's eggs may provide a source of essential nutrients useful for the production of the cuckoo's own eggs. With a mainly caterpillar diet, female cuckoos may be unable to extract sufficient minerals such as calcium for this purpose. Non-parasitic cuckoos also eat eggs and nest-lings of small birds, although it is not known whether this is confined only to females in their egg-laying periods. The fact that these species also rob nests suggests that such behaviour was common cuckoo practice prior to the evolution of brood parasitism.

Secondly, female cuckoos could deliberately destroy nests for which they have no further use, inferring a means by which cuckoos could manipulate the availability of nests suitable for parasitism. When hosts lose a nest they immediately set about building a new one. In the case of the small passerine hosts of the European Cuckoo, a new nest with the first egg can be produced in as little as four days. Occasionally, but not always, the repeat-nest will be parasitized. Any nest that has not been parasitized, or is not intended to be, may be predated and the host pair forced to build a new nest. A female Cuckoo can thus assure a supply of nests for her subsequent eggs. This pattern of behaviour has been a regular feature of Cuckoos parasitizing Reed Warblers at my study site but, as yet, I have never seen an individually marked female rob a nest and return to lay an egg in the repeat-nest.

During his study of Cuckoos and Meadow Pipits, Chance (1940) himself destroyed all the host nests once they had gone beyond a stage suitable for parasitism. In this way the dozen or so pairs of pipits on his common were constantly building new nests which the Cuckoos were parasitizing. His Cuckoo A laid as many as 25 eggs in one season, the maximum ever recorded for a parasitic cuckoo of any species. It is impossible to say whether this bird would have laid so many eggs if Chance had not experimentally provided a succession of nests, but she would have had either to rob nests herself, or travel about five kilometres to the nearest neighbouring pipits, or parasitize some other local host species.

Thirdly, robbing host nests could be a mechanism whereby rival females are prevented from laying in one another's egg-laying range. This is perhaps a rather unlikely tactic for which the evidence is only circumstantial. On a few occasions when I have watched rival female Cuckoos lay in the egg ranges of other females, I have noticed that a second female (presumed to be the 'owner' of the range) has been watching the proceedings from close by. The egg of the rival bird has often disappeared a few days later along with the host's eggs. On other occasions the rival egg has been exchanged for an egg of the second-laying female, usually within a day or two. Chance (1940) hinted that a female in occupation of a good egg-laying area could prevent other females using it, but he quoted an observation made by F. Simmonds who saw two female Cuckoos attacking each other during a simul-taneous egg-laying in two nests only about 25m apart. Both were successful in laying, but the outcome of the eggs would not have been known since all Cuckoo eggs were collected. Similarly, at my study site two females laid eggs on the same day in nests only 10m apart. In this instance both hatched and fledged. On another occasion I photographed a Cuckoo robbing one egg from a Reed Warbler nest. Ten minutes later a strange female to the area laid in a totally unsuitable Reed Warbler nest containing four eggs that were incubated by four days. The one-egg nest that was robbed was the only suitable nest in the vicinity and it was easy to infer that the dominant female had robbed that nest to prevent the stranger laying in her territory. Such an assumption, however, needs to be corroborated by more observations of marked birds.

Clearly host-nest predation can have many advantages to cuckoos but the precise function of it cannot be construed from the evidence at hand. Only by detailed observations of individually marked birds can any firmer conclusions be drawn.

Cuckoos as prey

Finally in this chapter on the food of cuckoos, it is worth mentioning that cuckoos themselves are liable to predation, mainly by raptorial birds. The European Cuckoo, for example, is not infrequent prey of Peregrine Falcon, *Falco peregrinus*, Goshawk, *Accipiter gentilis*, and Spar-rowhawk, *A. nisus*, and is killed to a lesser extent by kites, harriers, falcons and owls (Uttendorfer 1952). Young ones have been seen to be killed by Arctic Skuas, *Stercorarius parasiticus*, in the Shetlands (Meinertzhagen 1959).

Young cuckoos, parasitic or not, are subject to predation by any natural nest-robber. Non-parasitic cuckoos have evolved rapid nestling development as well as rapid embryonic development which counter such predation. They mostly have black skins covered with bristly 'hairs' which may deter predators. All young cuckoos also excrete special foul-smelling liquid faeces when attacked. Nevertheless, they are heavily predated by a wide range of nest predators. Nestling European

Cuckoos may be taken by Magpies, Jays, and other crows, but are probably more frequently killed by terrestrial mammals such as stoats, weasels and foxes. A young Cuckoo is at a special disadvantage as it grows and fills the host nest: the nest may start to disintegrate and the youngster fall to the ground, the longer time spent in the nest compared to the host young increases the chance of predation, and the loud food-begging calls can attract enemies from some distance. Once they have left the nest and reached the comparative safety of a nearby bush, young Cuckoos are less likely to be taken by predatory ground mammals but are more likely to fall victims to birds of prey, especially during the first few days until they can fly well.

It has been suggested that, through eating noxious caterpillars, cuckoos may be unpalatable, but this is without serious foundation. Young European Cuckoos are regarded as a great delicacy in Italy (they are fat there before migrating into Africa), and Payne (1974) ate several African cuckoos raw and found them quite edible!

5 | Songs and Calls

Throughout the world cuckoo species are probably better known by their calls rather than by their appearance. Almost all Europeans should be familiar with the song of the Cuckoo but many people have never seen one. All cuckoo species, parasites and nesters, have far-carrying and distinctive songs, and because of their persistent calling some have been nicknamed 'brain-fever birds'. In fact the songs of cuckoos have given rise to endless folklore and superstitions, none more so than the European bird (see Hardy 1879). Country folk in some areas still maintain that hearing the Cuckoo singing is a sign of imminent rain or bad weather. This is quite understandable in England because the Cuckoo arrives in April when there is a good chance of traditional showery weather. African species of cuckoos arrive and sing in their breeding ranges at the beginning of the wet season, and in India, Jacobin Cuckoos, *Clamator jacobinus*, for example, appear at the beginning of the monsoon. This close association with rainfall in the tropics is no coincidence: the rain promotes the growth of the foodplants of the cuckoo's food, and initiates breeding by most host species.

The songs of birds have two main, easily recognizable functions. They are usually given by the males to defend territories and to attract mates. Several male and female cuckoos may breed in the same area as one another, where each male attempts to court all the females as well as compete with rival males. Song is used extensively in both these activities.

Not only are cuckoo songs species-specific, they are also individualistic, so that each male recognizes its neighbours by small variations in pitch and tempo. When males first arrive in their breeding range, they eagerly investigate rivals' songs and aggressive encounters are frequent. About a week or so later this reaction relaxes, suggesting that each male has learnt the songs of its neighbours and no longer investigates birds which he has come to know personally. On the other hand, he will immediately investigate a newcomer.

Two birds seldom sing simultaneously, but rather one bird may sing for a few minutes and stop, then another take over, and so on. Alternatively, two birds may sing in 'harmony' with each call of one bird uttered during the interval of the other. Two males can keep such dueting up for many minutes without physical contact. It has long been assumed that this signifies strict territoriality in the species, but my observations on individually marked males have shown this not to be the case (see next chapter).

Lack (1968) presumed that the songs of parasitic cuckoos are simple because the young cannot learn them from their parents, but even non-parasitic cuckoo species have simple and distinctive songs. Mostly they consist of several syllables uttered at varying speed and volume, and persistently repeated. They are characteristically loud and far-carrying, often with a ventriloquial property making the singing bird difficult to locate. In these naturally secretive and skulking birds, songs or calls are often the only indication of their presence in an area.

Songs and calls of the European Cuckoo

Chance (1940) felt that his description of Cuckoo calls was unsatisfactory, but even today little advance can be made on his findings. He brought particular attention to the call of the female which was, and still is, generally poorly known and infrequently heard. He described the various calls as follows:

1   The bi-syllabic 'cuck-oo' call repeated about every 1–1.5 seconds constitutes the well-known song of the male. These calls usually number about 10–20 (up to 270 recorded) in an uninterrupted series, with a few seconds interval between series. During courtship it is not unusual to hear several 'cuck' calls to one 'oo', or vice versa. Commonly, however, such calls are 'cuck-cuck-oo'. It is possible that the female also uses the 'cuck-oo' call on occasions, but it has never been satisfactorily proven. Of the females watched by Chance, none was ever heard to call 'cuck-oo' and other students of breeding Cuckoos, including myself, have had a similar experience. There is an old record of a bird calling 'cuck-oo' being shot and found on dissection to be a female, but this is probably unreliable (Yapp 1962). Unless it can be shown otherwise by watching individually marked birds, the 'cuck-oo' will remain known as the exclusive call of the male.

2   Chance referred to the excited 'chuckle' of the male with which there should be no confusion with that of the female. This puzzled me for some time. On two occasions in 1975 I heard a male terminate its song with a 'bubble' exactly like that used by the female. Since the bird

was not in view I concluded that a female may have been responsible for these calls. It was not until three years later that I heard another male terminate his song with what I also described as a 'chuckle'. This was very similar to, but deeper and harsher than a female 'bubble'. As the bird was in full view, and was a marked male, there was no doubt that he used this call as well as the 'cuck-oo'. I presume that this was the call to which Chance referred but, allowing for individual variation in female calls, a degree of confusion between the two is likely. On another occasion I saw and heard another wing-tagged male give a perfect female-like 'bubbling' call while flying across an open field. Hickman (1975) saw two Cuckoos also in an open field which both used the 'cuck-oo' and 'bubble', but he had no idea whether these were two males, two females, or a pair.

3   The 'bubble' of the female was first fully described by Chance, and the term is now in popular use. He also described it as a 'hinny'. It consists of a single clear, liquid cry of about 15 notes on a descending scale and lasting about three seconds. Bubbling females are most likely to be heard in May and June, particularly after egg-laying. Occasionally a female may utter two or more bubbles in quick succession.

4   Chance referred to the 'mewing' by a female when watching prospective host nests or prior to laying. He stated that one needed to be very close to hear it, but none of the many females I have watched laying at close range in Reed Warbler nests have used the call. A similar call has been described for the American Yellow-billed Cuckoo, *Coccyzus americanus*, by Hamilton and Hamilton (1965) who recorded a 'special mewing call' as part of a distraction display when the nest was threatened.

5   A call used by both sexes and uttered mainly in flight or upon alighting was interpreted by Chance as 'wah-wah' repeated rapidly. This call is most often used when two or more birds are together. A male will sometimes prefix its song with a short, rather gruff, 'wah' or 'wah-wah', and two disputing males use this call aggressively between song calls. A female occasionally uses it when defying a rival, or when harassed by a male, or mobbed by some small bird.

6   Chance described a peculiar 'grorr-grorr-grorr' as a 'passionate utterance drawled out by the male when not in flight'. I think that this is a variation of (5) above.

7   Witherby *et al.* (1938) referred to a short, sharp, explosive hiss used to frighten small birds and by the male when chasing a female. Chance only quoted this reference, so presumably did not hear it. On one occasion in May, I saw two Cuckoos twisting and weaving rapidly through a small wood, apparently a male chasing a female in courtship.

One bird uttered a snake-like, but short repetitive hiss, although I could not tell whether it was male or female.

Delivery

A male Cuckoo delivers its song from almost any perch ranging from ground level to the top of a tall tree. A song post may be exposed, such as a wire, or the bird may be hidden in dense canopy foliage. When singing against another male, a bird generally faces the direction of its rival; experiments with tape-recordings show that, despite the ventriloquial quality, a male can accurately pin-point the direction of a song from up to about 1km away. Some authors claim the carrying power of the song to be as much as 5km, but in favourable conditions, about 1–1.5km is nearer the truth. Cuckoos frequently sing in flight and often start just before alighting. They are also well-known to sing at night, as are many cuckoo species around the world.

The bubbling call of the female is also delivered in flight or from a suitable perch. At close range the feathers of the throat can be seen to vibrate. The precise function of the call is difficult to establish as it may be heard at any time during the breeding season, and even on migration in Africa (Moreau 1972). The call is almost invariably used before and after egg-laying: so much so that if it is heard in the afternoon or early evening in the breeding season it is highly probable that an egg has been, or is about to be, laid. The female calls of other species of cuckoo are imperfectly known, but it would seem that the bubbling note occurs in at least other *Cuculus* species.

Seasonality

Male Cuckoos begin to sing as soon as they arrive in the breeding range in spring. In Britain, song can be heard mainly from late April until the end of June or early July, and only rarely in August. The amount of song varies between seasons. At my study site in 1975–1979, I consistently recorded the amount of time that males were heard singing in relation to the amount of time I spent in the field (Figure 4). For example, in the ten days from the arrival of the first male in 1975, I spent 1,605 minutes in the field during which male song was heard in 890 minutes or for 55 per cent of the time. On average over the five years males sang most when they first arrived. After a week or so, and at about the time the females arrived, song output usually decreased. Possibly at this time males had exhausted supplies of any surplus fat with which they arrived and were spending more time foraging. Also one of the functions of song

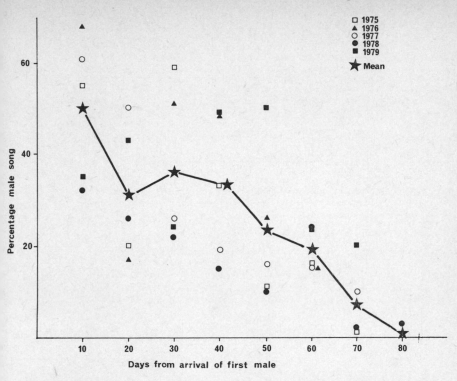

Figure 4. Male Cuckoo song output as proportion of field recording time in Cambridgeshire, 1975–1979

(mate attraction) had been fulfilled. Generally, song output increased during the pre-laying period, usually in mid-May, with a noticeable decline in most years just before the first eggs were laid. Thereafter song output usually declined until departure. I could find no correlation between seasonal variation in song output and weather. I suspected that song increased when food was plentiful and decreased at times of shortage, but I could make no assessment of food abundance.

Table 14 indicates the seasonal presence of Cuckoos at the site based on earliest and latest vocalizations. Except in 1976, a season of severe drought when few eggs were produced despite an abundance of host nests, males usually stopped singing before the last eggs were laid each year. The total amount of song heard compared to the time I spent in the field averaged 28 per cent over the five years. Generally, in years of good egg production (1974, 1975, 1978, 1979), male song extended over 9 or 10 weeks, whereas in years of poor egg production (1976, 1977) song lasted only 8 or 9 weeks. Female calls also extended over a 9- or 10-week

Table 14 *Amount of Cuckoo,* Cuculus canorus, *vocalization at Cambridgeshire study site 1974–1979*

	Males					Females								
Year	no. present*	earliest	latest	no. days	% output**	no. present†	no. calls recorded	earliest	latest	no. days	calls/ hour	latest egg	no. eggs	% nests parasitized
1974	–	28.4	10.7	74	–	6	78	4.5	14.7	72	–	11.7	26	23
1975	5	19.4	30.6	73	25	8	131	2.5	9.7	69	0.24	8.7	35	16
1976	4	4.5	27.6	55	39	3	41	21.5	25.6	38	0.22	9.6	5	4
1977	5	28.4	28.6	62	25	3	17	10.5	28.6	50	0.05	29.6	6	3
1978	4	1.5	11.7	72	24	3	78	4.5	14.7	72	0.22	14.7	24	11
1979	7	6.5	7.7	63	34	3	157	11.5	8.7	59	0.39	11.7	23	9

* Number of males present each year based on song registrations, simultaneous song, individual variations in song, and individually marked birds.
** Song output as a percentage of minutes in the field in which males heard singing.
† Number of females based on number of egg-types (ie. only includes breeding birds).

period in the years of good egg-production, but for only 6 or 7 weeks in poor years. The total number of calls heard each year in relation to time spent (i.e. equivalent to male song output), averaged 0.27 calls per hour, roughly one call for every four hours spent in the field. Like male song output, the amount of female calling varied from year to year with no clear correlation with weather. Female calling was also very variable during the course of each season (Table 15), but was generally more noticeable in the main laying period from late May to mid-June.

Daily use of song and calls

Males at my study site were most vocal in the early morning (0400–0800 hours BST) throughout the breeding season (Figure 5). In mid-summer Cuckoos were among the earliest birds to initiate the dawn chorus, starting about one hour before sunrise. They were also one of the last to sing at night – up to one hour after sunset. I did not hear birds at night, although this is a frequently reported occurrence as mentioned above.

Diurnal song output is probably influenced by many factors such as time of season, female or male activity, food availability, and the weather. A typical daily song cycle, like other birds, consists of a period of intensive song around daybreak, then a stop presumably to feed. Singing may be sporadic during the late morning and afternoon, becoming more pronounced in the late afternoon during the laying period. Song output tends to increase again at dusk prior to roosting.

Figure 5 also shows the number of female calls recorded each year at different times of day. In almost every year, females were also most vocal in the early morning, particularly during the arrival and courtship period in May. Calls later in the morning were mainly associated with incidents of host-nest predation (see Chapter 4). Afternoon bubbles (1200–1900 hours BST) were heard only in the laying period from late May until mid-July. Evening calls (1900–2200 hours BST) were heard when females joined males at roost.

Reactions by other birds

Other bird species inhabiting the same areas as Cuckoos can hardly fail to recognize their presence. Most of them seem to take no interest at all. Some species of songbirds can mimic the female bubbling call to perfection. At my study site a male Song Thrush, *Turdus philomelos*, which held a territory for three years in an area where Cuckoo activity was very strong, imitated the bubbling call so well that I always had to check that

Table 15   *Seasonal use of female Cuckoo, Cuculus canorus, calls at study site in Cambridgeshire, 1974–1979*

Year (first female call)	No. females	Number of calls in 10 day periods									
		21–30.4	1–10.5	11–20.5	21–31.5	1–10.6	11–20.6	21–30.6	1–10.7	11–20.7	TOTAL
1974 (4.5)	6	–	1	–	9	20	26	6	7	9	78
1975 (2.5)	8	–	12	15	53	21	13	11	6	–	131
1976 (21.5)	3	–	–	–	24	12	4	1	–	–	41
1977 (10.5)	3	–	1	1	3	8	1	3	–	–	17
1978 (4.5)	3	–	21	4	3	11	25	10	–	4	78
1979 (11.5)	3	–	–	53	3	40	46	11	4	–	157
		–	35	73	95	112	115	42	17	13	502
Mean		–	5.8	12.2	15.8	18.7	19.2	7.0	2.8	2.2	

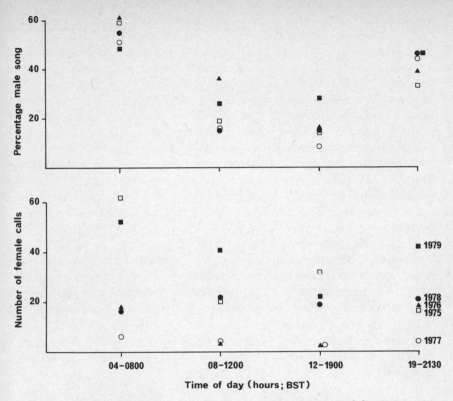

Figure 5. Amount of Cuckoo vocalization according to time of day in Cambridgeshire, 1975–1979

he was not singing when I heard the call. Similarly, and perhaps ironically, one male Reed Warbler also incorporated a perfect bubble in its song repertoire. It is debatable whether host species recognize female Cuckoo calls which they hear only infrequently, but they undoubtedly recognize the male's song and some species react accordingly. Willow Warblers, *Phylloscopus trochilus*, for instance, not only will attack just the head of a Cuckoo placed near their nest as demonstrated by Smith and Hosking (1955), they also respond aggressively to tape-recordings of Cuckoo song played near the nest. In conjunction with a stuffed Cuckoo these birds lose all fear of man in their attempts to attack the parasite (black and white photograph 13).

Calls of young cuckoos

The first call uttered by a Cuckoo is, of course, the food-begging call used by the nestling during the host-dependence period. At first, from about 24 hours old, this is a thin, squeeky 'seep' which is used only when a foster parent arrives with food. This gradually gets louder until, at about seven days old, it is audible for several metres and becomes more persistent. At a fortnight old the young Cuckoo emits a single chirp repeated at few-second intervals when the hosts are away collecting food. As they approach the nest with food this chirp becomes louder and more frequent until, when being fed, it becomes a loud, rapid-repeated hiss which is audible for about 50 metres. The youngster uses these calls for the rest of the time it remains dependent upon the hosts. Their loudness and persistence, coupled with the red-orange gape, seem to attract other birds in the neighbourhood from which the youngster solicits more food. The calls also attract predators which account for a high mortality in young Cuckoos (see Chapter 10). If handled at this stage the youngster emits a harsh, rattling, hawk-like alarm call.

Constant calling for food from the nest after two weeks when the hosts' young would normally have fledged, perhaps acts as an essential stimulus to prolong the nestling-care period of the host pair and is presumably more important than remaining silent to try to avoid predation.

Courtney (1967) noted that the juvenile food-begging calls of some fledgling Australian cuckoos seemed to mimic those of their hosts even though they were reared alone. He suggested that different host-specific strains of parasite cuckoos could be maintained, not only by egg-mimicry, but also by such vocal mimicry. He observed that the young Pallid Cuckoo, *Cuculus pallidus*, mimicked the food-begging call of young White-eared Honeyeaters, *Glycichaera fallax*, one of the main hosts, while Serventy and Whittel (1962) had reported that this young Cuckoo sounded like young Red Wattle-Birds *Anthochaera carunculata*, a common host in the southwest. Similarly, for the Great Spotted Cuckoo, *Clamator glandarius*, Mundy (1973) reported that the young sounded like young Pied Crows, *Corvus albus* in sub-Saharan Africa, but in southwest Africa, like young Pale-winged Starlings, *Onycognathus nabouroup*, and in Europe, like young Magpies, *Pica pica*. These observations suggest that, where a young cuckoo is reared along with all or some of the host young, vocal mimicry may have evolved through natural selection by discriminating host species. Hence, young which sound like the young of the particular host species are more likely to be accepted and reared. This does not seem to have happened in cuckoo species where the host young are ejected or killed by the young cuckoo soon after hatching. In the European Cuckoo, for example, which has many different host species, there appear to be no regional, racial or host-specific differences in the food-begging calls of the young.

The parasitic widowbirds (Viduinae) in Africa have taken vocal mimicry by their young one evolutionary step further: the males learn and copy the songs of their respective hosts and females only mate with males of their own species sounding like their respective foster-fathers. This is one way in which each species of widowbird remains host-specific – a vitally important strategy if the young are to survive.

6 | The Social System

One of my main objectives in studying an individually marked population of cuckoos was to investigate territoriality, courtship and pair-formation. Did Cuckoos have territories which they defended against rivals, and did they form pair-bonds during the breeding season? Nobody had worked with a population of marked birds before. Regrettably, it proved impossible to catch and wing-tag all the birds at my study site each season, so I had to be content with plotting the movements of a few marked birds, along with those of males with recognizable songs. An attempt to assess the laying areas occupied by individual females could be made by plotting the distribution of their unique eggs.

Territoriality

Because of their persistent songs given from regular song posts, male Cuckoos are widely regarded as territorial birds, and vocal arguments or physical combats between males have been interpreted as territorial disputes. My observations on marked birds soon showed that this was not strictly the case: two or more males used exactly the same song posts during the course of a breeding season, though not at the same time. I also found that their ranges overlapped with one another over most of the observed area (Figure 6). For over half the time I spent in the field, males were silent and nowhere to be found; they were only conspicuous near the reedbeds where eggs were laid. I presumed they travelled elsewhere to gather most of their food. The distance covered was too great and encounters with marked birds were too few to allow an accurate assessment of an individual male's total range in the breeding season.

In 1979, I put radio transmitters on three adult males caught in the laying area in the hope of plotting their ranges over the next few weeks. The first bird was caught on 13 May, but the transmitter came off the next day before it had moved. The second was caught on 16 May and the following day I followed it 4km to an orchard where it fed most of the day. On 18 May it returned to its place of capture where it was seen to associate with another male, sing occasionally, and feed on the ground below a row of mature trees. In the afternoon it moved about 2km to another reedbed site where it sang, on and off, until dusk. On 19 May it again travelled to the orchard, but returned to the second reedbed by evening. During the night it was killed by a Tawny Owl, *Strix aluco*, which fed it to its large chick; I retrieved the transmitter, still sending out its signal, from the owl's nest two days later. The third male was caught at this second reedbed on 22 May when it responded to tape-recordings of the female bubble and the sight of a stuffed specimen, to which, incidentally, it presented plant material (see below). Later in the day it sang and roosted about 1km away. It remained here, in an area of meadows surrounded by mature hedges away from the reedbeds, until 26 May. Then it disappeared until 5 June when it was heard singing in the same place. On 6 June it came to another reedbed about 1km from its place of capture, but was immediately chased off by an unmarked male. Until 13 June I found it in the usual hedges where it seemed to spend nearly all the time feeding, only singing very occasionally. On 15 June it moved about another 1km to a new feeding place; thereafter I lost track of it and presumed the transmitter had failed or that the Cuckoo moved away again. During the three weeks under my observation, therefore, this male spent most of its time feeding away from the reedbeds to which it only came twice to my knowledge. It rarely sang and, as far as I knew, did not associate with any females; I concluded that it was a non-breeding bird.

These observations on marked and radio-tracked birds suggest that male Cuckoos sing mainly in areas where females lay their eggs; each male may sing in an area of about 30 hectares, but travel at least 4km away to feed. Taking 4km as the minimum diameter of a circle representing an hypothetical Cuckoo range would mean a bird occupying 1,257 hectares.

The fact that my males overlapped with one another so extensively in both song-ranges and feeding-ranges makes it doubtful whether they were at all territorial. Rather, I suggest, there was a hierarchical social system or 'peck-order' in which dominant males expelled subordinate birds whenever they came in contact in the potential laying areas. Contacts were few because males spent most of the time feeding quietly and alone, away from the laying-sites. In Cuckoos parasitizing other host species, especially those which are more evenly spaced in the environment, territory may be more important. Cuckoos parasitizing Meadow Pipits, for example, are possibly more spread out because their hosts, unlike Reed Warblers, are not concentrated in small areas. However, Chance found more than one pair of Cuckoos on his 25-

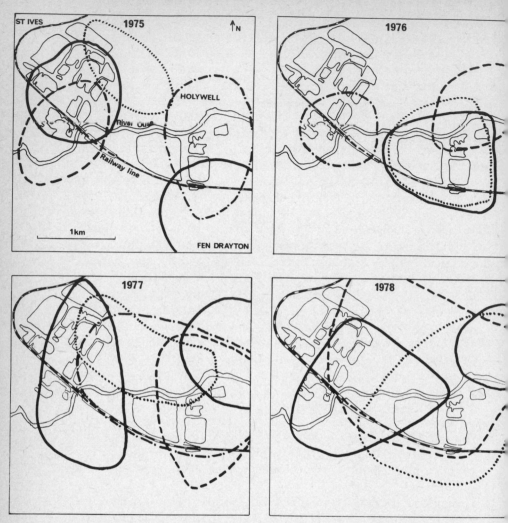

Figure 6. Map of main study site at St Ives, Cambridgeshire, showing male song ranges in 1975–1978

hectare common in each season. The males appeared only infrequently, and he also thought they spent most of their time feeding in the surrounding woodland and orchards.

Another problem is that some birds, possibly in their first year, have no fixed area. These could travel widely, and stop off at many places for varying periods of time, making it almost impossible to count the number of males in one area.

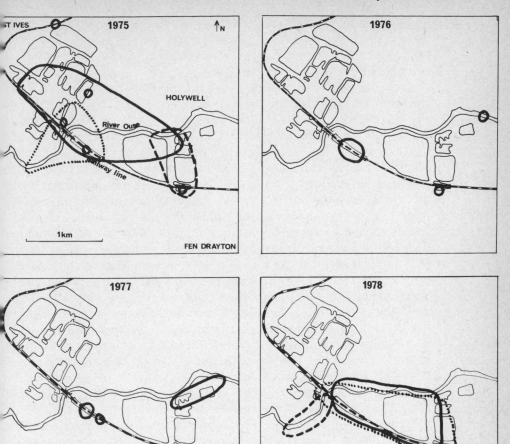

Figure 7. Map of main study site at St Ives, Cambridgeshire, showing female egg-laying ranges in 1975–1978

The evidence for separate female 'territories' or rather, egg-laying ranges, is more pronounced. Firstly, it is rare for two females to lay in the same nest (see Chapter 8). Secondly, field studies have shown that females tend to have separate egg-ranges, particularly when the hosts are widely spaced. Chance's Cuckoo A was thought to have laid 90 eggs in five years when only 7 eggs of two other females were found in Meadow Pipit nests on the same common. He deduced that Cuckoo A was a dominant bird which prevented rival females from parasitizing 'her' nests. Later, however, in 1927–1930, two females shared the common laying 19 and 13 eggs respectively in Meadow Pipit nests. Perhaps these birds were of equal status.

At my main study site in Cambridgeshire in 1974–1979, there were at least three females laying in any one year. Only twice at this particular site did two females lay in the same nest (see Chapter 8) but I recorded this at another four nests at other sites. Despite this mainly individual use of host nests, the laying areas of particular females overlapped with others, almost as much as did male song ranges. In one year (1975), three females laid into different Reed Warbler nests only 30m apart, and on another occasion (in 1978), two Cuckoos laid on the same afternoon in nests only 10m apart. Figure 7 illustrates the egg-laying ranges of female Cuckoos at my main study site in 1975–1978, corresponding with Figure 6 of male song ranges. There was perhaps a stronger tendency towards separate egg ranges in 1975 when eight females laid 35 eggs between them. One bird (code name 75P) laid 10 eggs in an area of about 30 hectares. She laid another about three-quarters of a kilometre away, into a previously parasitized nest in the range of another bird (74B), removing the original Cuckoo egg in the process. She laid another egg in the range of a third female (75C) about one and a half kilometres away. The two 'invaded' ranges were also about 30 hectares in extent, and were about 1.2km apart. These two females each laid 9 eggs. Five other females in 1975 laid only single eggs, all but one within the egg-laying ranges of the three more prolific birds. The two years 1976 and 1977 were poor egg-production years, and the three females in each laid apart. In 1978, however, the two most productive females, laying 15 and 6 eggs respectively, used the same area, though not the same nests. Other studies of egg-laying ranges in European Cuckoos have shown a tendency towards isolation of females, but there is nearly always some non-exclusive area.

The movements of a female followed by radio telemetry in 1979 illustrate, in perhaps more detail than ever before, the range of one Cuckoo during part of its breeding season (Figure 8). This bird (code name 79C) was caught with a male at a reedbed laying site on the evening of 13 May. I released both birds at the same place next morning. The female did not move far until the afternoon of the following day when I lost her. Two days later (17 May) a radio-tracked male, mentioned above, led me to the feeding place – an orchard and area of railway scrub about 4km from where I had caught female 79C. She apparently spent all her time here until 25 May, when she at last visited the two reedbed sites where she was to lay all her eggs. On 27 May she

26 At two days old the young Cuckoo is now the sole occupant of the nest and weighs about 8 g

27 By the time it is four days old the young Cuckoo fills the bottom of the nest and now weighs as much as one of its Reed Warbler fosterparents

28 At six days old the feathers begin to emerge and the eyes open

29 At 12 days old the young Cuckoo appears well-feathered. It is now no longer brooded by its fosterparents and may succumb to bad weather, or fall from the nest, or be found by a predator

30 Even when just fed the young Cuckoo continues to gape and call for more food. The psychological stimulus of the red gape and constant begging cries ensure that the hosts do not desert

31 When 16 days old the young Cuckoo completely fills the nest and dwarfs its Reed Warbler fosterparent

32 The young Cuckoo requires a high protein diet such as this beakful of flies brought by a Reed Warbler. Cuckoos are rarely, if ever, reared by host species which do not bring insects to their young

33 At 18 days old a young Cuckoo raises one wing which it quivers while being fed

34 After it leaves the nest, the young Cuckoo seeks the safety of a nearby bush in which it demands food from any passing bird. It remains dependent upon the hosts for a further three weeks

35 A Dunnock has to stand on the young Cuckoo's back in order to reach its gaping mouth

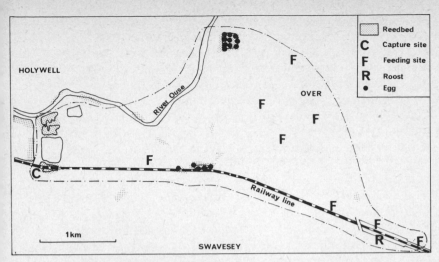

Figure 8. Area occupied by female Cuckoo 79C followed by radio-telemetry at Over, Cambridgeshire, in 1979

visited another reedbed near her place of capture, and I could see her watching two Reed Warbler nests under construction. However, she laid no eggs there, nor did she revisit her place of capture. On the following day (28 May) she was very active, commuting from one laying site to the other, and to her roosting and feeding place on the railway. She probably laid her first egg of the season on this day in a Sedge Warbler, *Acrocephalus schoenobaenus*, nest, but I did not find the egg – only the young Cuckoo later in June. (I could accurately estimate the laying-date from the age of the young Cuckoo.) Thereafter she laid at two-day intervals from 30 May until 11 June, always in Reed Warbler nests at one or other of the laying sites. Although present at one site for most of the afternoon on 13 June, she did not lay. From then on, I could not afford the time to follow her activities quite so closely; but she continued to lay only at these two places until 10 July (see Chapter 8), and to feed at the railway scrub site or in orchards nearby where there were plenty of caterpillars. At each of the three main areas used by this Cuckoo from 13 May until 10 July (i.e. the two egg-laying sites and the main feeding place where she also roosted), there were different males present. In total, to my knowledge alone, this one female came into contact with six males during the breeding season. However, I did not see her mated by any of them. There were also at least three other females using the same feeding and roost site, and from their egg-types, three other females also laid at the same egg-laying sites. Such a distribution of individuals could hardly be described as territorial. Edgar Chance also concluded that a hierarchical or dominancy system prevented prolific females from laying their eggs into the same nests. He thought that females avoided using the same nests by physically defending 'their' nests against rivals, but he recorded only one instance of a female fighting with another; in this case both birds laid in separate pipit nests only 27m apart. Baker also believed that dominant females tried to maintain exclusive use of their particular host species' nests, but that females parasitizing other host species in the same area could be tolerated. This seems most improbable since all female Cuckoos look alike regardless of their choice of host. It seems unlikely that a female could identify the host to be used by another female using the same area.

Why then is it rare to find more than one Cuckoo egg in a nest? The answer may lie in host-nest predation behaviour of each dominant female. I mentioned earlier (Chapter 4) that the eggs of rival females often disappeared soon after they were laid and that females occasionally watched others laying. The activities of female 79C in early June when she laid 8 eggs in series are of particular interest in this respect. Remember that the two places where she laid her 15 eggs were also used by three other Cuckoos for 11 of their eggs. As far as I knew, female 79C robbed no nests until 3 June, the same day that a rival female (79OB) started laying in the same area. Female 79C was seen to rob nests (other than the ones in which she laid) on four of her laying days. On 5 and 11 June she laid into nests previously used by female 79B, removing the first laid Cuckoo egg each time. On 2 July she laid in a nest in which two days earlier another female (79GB) had laid, but this time she did not remove the Cuckoo egg. The final outcome of the 11 'stranger' eggs was that 5 disappeared along with the host clutch, 2 were eaten by 79C when she laid in the same nests, and 4 hatched, one of the young ejecting another of 79C's eggs because it hatched first. Possibly, this female Cuckoo tried to stop rivals using the same nests by robbing ones used by other females and for which she had no use herself.

Pair-formation

A comparison of Figures 6 and 7 shows that, not only did male song-ranges overlap with one another and female egg-ranges were not separate, but several males and females occupied mutual areas. With such a distribution pattern within the sexes, the possibility of true pair-formation seems rather unlikely. Chance guessed that Cuckoos paired, even for life, but he produced no evidence for this, and noted that more than one male occasionally accompanied his female Cuckoo

A. Many other observers have noted more than one male (up to four or five) accompanying a female, but none have worked on individually marked birds or seen mating frequently enough to clarify the situation. Nearly every female that I studied in Cambridgeshire in six years was courted by more than one male in the same season, and where a female returned for more than one year, she was invariably seen with different males, some of which were marked. In fact one female was courted by its own offspring: a male wing-tagged in the nest in 1975 and seen in the following three years as a breeding bird.

Because males are more conspicuous, it has been thought that they outnumber the females so that polyandry is the rule in the Cuckoo's social system. Detailed studies at breeding sites, however, have shown that there may in fact be more females than males. This raises the possibility that males are polygamous. Since song areas and egg ranges overlap so largely, at least at my study site where Reed Warblers were the hosts, I favour the idea that Cuckoos are promiscuous. Other species in the world are also thought to have promiscuous mating systems, while some may be polygamous, polyandrous or monogamous. Monogamy is inferred in those species where both partners are involved in the process of parasitizing nests. Since no other species has been studied on an individually marked basis, the evidence for any pairing system in parasitic cuckoos remains inconclusive, and further research is again desperately needed in this field.

Some young Cuckoos return to their natal areas to breed in later life. If they do not return to their birthplaces, they might at least breed in similar habitats where there are the same host species. Thus a young Cuckoo reared in a Meadow Pipit nest on a Scottish hillside might return to another hillside where Meadow Pipits breed. Or a young Cuckoo from a Rock Pipit nest on the Scilly Isles may return, not to the same island, but to a similar habitat where there are Rock Pipits. In this way the gene for host-specificity could be kept distinct and a promiscuous mating system need not harm the inheritance mechanism for egg-mimicry (see Chapters 7 and 9).

Courtship and mating

The principle element of courtship in Cuckoos, as discussed in the last chapter, is male song. Song is accompanied by posturing, display flights, presentation of plant material, and possibly courtship feeding. The female attracts a male with the bubbling call. A male approaches in song and alights nearby with wings hanging, head bowed and tail held erect and fanned to expose the white markings. The tail is rotated slowly and the body swayed from side to side in this typical display posture. Occasionally the male drops to the ground to collect a small stick or leaf which he holds in his bill for several seconds. Transfer of such material has never been witnessed, but Chance (1940, p. 52) claimed to have seen a female circling above the common on 1 May carrying a 15cm twig or straw while being pursued by a singing male. Numerous observers have seen male Cuckoos apparently presenting such material to females, mainly in late April or early May, the main courtship period.

There are two special styles of flight associated with courtship. Firstly, there is a swift, darting and weaving flight performed when a male chases a prospective mate. This could be a way of assessing a male's fitness: if he can keep up with the female, she may accept him – if not, he is rejected. Since the female is courted by several males during a breeding season, this style of flight could be one way of sorting 'the men from the boys'. The second display flight is soaring during which both partners circle high in the air on outstretched wings. When two males simultaneously court or chase a female, they usually end up fighting with one another and the female slips off secretively, avoiding them both. The situation in Reed Warbler-Cuckoos would appear that the males only sing and look for the females in the places where they lay their eggs. The females, therefore, have to receive the attention of males, locate the host nests and lay their eggs at the laying sites: no wonder they are secretive and difficult to observe at such places.

Copulation in Cuckoos is a rarely witnessed event, this further impeding an assessment of the social organization. I have seen it only three times in six years of intensive observations, even using radio-telemetry to keep close track of one female. The three instances occurred on 6 and 8 June 1975 and 15 June 1979. They took place in the afternoon at the sites where the females laid their eggs, and both females concerned laid eggs later on the same day. Of course, the mating did not fertilize the egg laid on the same day. The first occasion concerned a wing-tagged female (75C) which appeared on top of a small bush overlooking a reedbed at 1304 hours BST on 6 June. This was my first encounter with the bird since her capture at the same site on 24 May. An unmarked male approached by gliding over a hedge and singing in flight. The female sat silently with tail depressed. The male landed directly on her back and copulation took place in three or four seconds. The pair flew off together, the male singing until 1330 hours. Later in the day, at 2000 hours, because I had delayed her somewhat by putting up hides, female 75C laid her first egg of the season in a Reed Warbler nest not 30m from the bush where mating occurred. The second occasion was two days later involving the same female and probably the same male at the same site. During the afternoon female 75C was seen to patrol her egg-laying range, and watched a rival female lay within it (she did not steal this bird's egg, however). At 1848 hours, eight minutes after the rival female laid, 75C flew to a dead branch overlooking the reedbed where she had laid two days ago. The singing male approached quite unexpectedly with gliding flight, landed directly on her back, and mating again took place in a few seconds. This time the male settled in a nearby bush and began singing vigorously, while the female bubbled. The male postured to her and they both flew to the ground where he picked up and dropped small twigs and leaves while constantly singing. He made mock attacks at the female, and she bubbled profusely until he stopped singing at 1926 hours. Then she glided around the reedbed making repeated stops near Reed Warbler nests that were only under construction. She was obviously getting desperate to lay. At 2055 hours she arrived at one half-built nest and stabbed her bill into it in apparent frustration. Five minutes later she finally bubbled, presumably having wasted the egg that was surely being carried in the oviduct.

The final occasion, on 15 June 1979, involved another female and unmarked male at one of the subsidiary sites surveyed. Copulation again occurred in a few seconds at 1410 hours on an exposed branch overlooking the reedbed where the female laid most of her eggs, including one later that day. Chance (1940) mentioned only one copulation incident which happened at 0815 hours on 5 June 1922, again a laying day. In Hungary, Molnar (1944) claimed that mating could occur at any time of day, often at dawn. He reported one instance at 0800 hours on 19 June. How frequently copulation occurs in Cuckoos is, at present, impossible to tell.

7 | Hosts

Brood parasitic birds have particular requirements in their selection of hosts. Generally, a host needs to be fairly common and breeding at the same time as the parasite. The nest or clutch must be accessible, the eggs of similar size and incubation period, and the host must accept the parasite's egg. Lastly, the host must provide a diet suitable for rearing the young parasite. If a host lacks just one of these features it will be relatively immune to parasitism.

Brood parasites are generally scarce birds enjoying an almost world-wide distribution and breeding seasons which coincide with maximum food availability, when most potential hosts breed. The breeding seasons of parasites and their hosts are presumably initiated by the same photo-periodic or environmental factors. Likely hosts, therefore, cannot avoid living in the same area or nesting at the same time as the parasites. But they can avoid parasitism by protecting their nests, eggs and young, and in these respects many birds have elaborate defences against parasitic birds. On their part, the parasites have countered some of these defences in remarkable ways.

Host defences against parasitic birds

One thing a potential host can do to avoid parasitism is to lay eggs which cannot be found or where a parasite cannot get its own eggs. Most insectivorous birds build hidden nests such as in holes or camouflaged in bushes. Others build exposed nests with tiny entrances, often with tunnels and hidden egg-chambers. Still others nest colonially relying on 'safety in numbers'. These strategies probably evolved as anti-predator defences and are still mainly effective as such, but they also function as anti-parasite mechanisms.

Secondly, a potential host can closely guard its nest against parasites, attacking any that come near. Many small birds mob European Cuckoos using special displays or alarm calls which attract neighbouring birds to the scene. Group mobbing, involving several species, may be more effective in deterring parasitic birds. If such a defence is unsuccessful, many birds will violently attack Cuckoos which approach their nests. In Hungary Molnar (1944) found several dead and dying female Cuckoos in the water below nests of Great Reed Warblers, which he presumed had succumbed to the attacks by the hosts. One of these warblers weighs about a quarter of the weight of a Cuckoo, so only four birds could theoretically overpower a laying female. These defences work sometimes but are not totally effective.

If the parasite manages to introduce its egg into the nest, there are several actions a host can take. Firstly, it may simply desert the nest. Since parasitic birds usually lay when the host is in the process of completing a clutch, desertion at this stage is not costly; the host can abort the nesting attempt, resorb any developing ova, and build a new nest ready for a new clutch in a very short time (about a week in passerine hosts of the Cuckoo). What often happens, however, is that the host completes its clutch, being unable to resorb eggs that are too far developed, and deserts a few days later. Another method is to build up the nest over the parasite's egg, burying it (and any host eggs that have been laid) below a new nest-lining, and then starting again. Nests of Reed Warblers, for example, have been found with two or more Cuckoo eggs buried at varying depths in the nest material. It is usually impossible to say whether a nest has been deserted because of being parasitized or because of some other cause. Consequently, it is not easy to quantify the proportion of parasitized nests which are deserted by different host species. Parasitized nests found by Baker (1942) in India were recorded as deserted or in occupation on discovery and, although this produced a strong bias (deserted nests were less likely to be found than occupied ones), Baker was able to show that desertion was more common in unusual hosts than in regular ones. Some of his examples are shown in Table 16, with additional data from other sources in Europe. The results indicate that frequent hosts of the Cuckoo did not abandon their nests when parasitized as often as did unusual host species. My own results in Cambridgeshire in 1974–1979 suggested a very low desertion percentage (2.9 per cent) by Reed Warblers, but this was based on parasitized nests in which eggs were definitely abandoned (i.e. with cold eggs in the nest on a subsequent visit). There were many cases (33 out of 170) where the whole parasitized clutch, or even the entire nest as well, had disappeared on a later visit: these probably included deserted nests and nests which were robbed first but dismantled by the hosts to rebuild elsewhere. There was no way of separating them. If these were regarded as all desertions, the total proportion of parasitized nests that were deserted becomes 22 per cent (38 out of 170).

Table 16 *Proportions of parasitized nests deserted by different hosts of Cuckoos, Cuculus canorus*

Subspecies	Host species	Region	No. of parasitized nests	No. deserted	%	Source
	(a) Frequent					
C.c. bakeri	Fantail Warbler, *Cisticola juncidis*	India	349	41	11.7	Baker 1942
	Hill warblers, *Suya* spp	India	348	31	8.9	Baker 1942
	Flycatchers	India	180	14	7.8	Baker 1942
	Pipits, *Anthus*	India	257	18	7.0	Baker 1942
	Other warblers	India	159	14	8.8	Baker 1942
	Thrushes	India	107	5	4.7	Baker 1942
	Mesia and Pekin Robin, *Leiothrix* spp	India	113	8	7.1	Baker 1942
C.c. telephonus	Rufous-backed Shrike, *Lanius collurioides*	India	21	3	14.3	Baker 1942
C.c. canorus	Redstart, *Phoenicurus phoenicurus*	Germany	88	5	5.7	Capek 1896
	Dunnock, *Prunella modularis*	England	302	1	0.3	Owen 1933
		England	25	0	0	Jourdain 1925
		Netherlands	41	2	4.9	Paulussen 1957
	Robin, *Erithacus rubeculla*	France	22	3	13.6	Blaise 1965

		England	89	4	4.5	Owen 1933
	Pied Wagtail, *Motacilla alba*	England	89	4	4.5	Owen 1933
	Red-backed Shrike, *Lanius collurio*	Germany	40	4	10.0	Capek 1896
(b) Less frequent or rare						
C.c. bakeri	Babblers, *Timalidae*	India	167	35	20.9	Baker 1942
	Treecreepers, *Certhia* etc.	India	30	4	13.3	Baker 1942
	Flycatchers, *Muscicapa*	India	30	9	30.0	Baker 1942
	Thrushes, *Turdidae*	India	27	7	25.9	Baker 1942
	Sparrows, *Passer*, etc.	India	25	13	52.0	Baker 1942
	Warblers, *Sylvidae*	India	19	4	21.0	Baker 1942
	Shrikes, *Laniidae*	India	82	29	35.4	Baker 1942
C.c. canorus	Wood Warbler, *Phylloscopus sibilatrix*	France	3	3	100	Blaise 1965
		Germany	17	13	76.5	Capek 1896
	Chiffchaff, *Phylloscopus collybita*	Germany	5	5	100	Walter 1889
	Whitethroat, *Sylvia communis*	Denmark	8	8	100	K. Barcord in Jourdain 1925
	Marsh Warbler, *Acrocephalus palustris*	Netherlands	30	6	20.0	Paulussen 1957
	Sedge Warbler, *Acrocephalus schoenobaenus*	Netherlands	17	3	17.6	Paulussen 1957
	Yellow Wagtail, *Motacilla flava*	Netherlands	16	1	6.2	Paulussen 1957
	Wren, *Troglodytes troglodytes*	Germany	44	21	47.7	Walter 1889

On the same basis, 7.6 per cent (91 out of 1,197) of unparasitized Reed Warbler nests were deserted where eggs were found cold, or 37 per cent (42.6 out of 1,197) if including cases where nests or whole clutches disappeared. These figures suggest that desertion of their nests by Reed Warblers was not influenced by the presence of Cuckoo eggs.

Another form of defence demands accurate egg-discrimination by the host, allowing ejection of the parasite's egg. If the host can recognize the strange egg, it can break it or throw it out. This was experimentally demonstrated long ago by Swynnerton (1918), Rensch (1924) and Ali (1931), who each placed strange eggs into the nests of potential cuckoo hosts and recorded the outcome. Many birds either deserted or ejected the introduced egg. One species, a Garden Warbler, *Sylvia borin*, actually removed one of its own eggs in favour of an introduced clutch of Lesser Whitethroat, *Sylvia curruca*, eggs. In other words, because its own egg looked the odd one in the clutch it threw it out. Similar experiments with captive African Village Weaverbirds, *Ploceus cucullatus* (a host of the Didric Cuckoo), showed that individual females could recognize their own eggs, and would eject introduced eggs from other members of their species (Victoria 1972).

When all else has failed and the parasite's egg hatches, the hosts can ignore the alien youngster so that it dies, but this is rarely recorded and difficult to prove and requires strict discriminatory powers on the part of the hosts which are better used on eggs than young.

Counters by parasitic birds to host defences

Nest-concealment does not prevent parasitic birds from locating and successfully parasitizing a wide range of hosts. Birds which nest in thick cover, in holes or cavities, or build domed, suspended or camouflaged nests, or those which nest colonially, may be safer than might otherwise be the case, but they are still susceptible to parasitism. The parasites, especially cuckoos, show remarkable versatility in their ability to lay eggs into this wide range of nest-types. The European Cuckoo, for example, can lay in the open nests of Reed Warblers which are delicately supported by reeds often over water, or into Dunnock nests hidden in low, dense herbage, into the domed nests of Wrens, or into the nests of Pied Wagtails, Rock Pipits or Redstarts in shallow cavities or crannies. In the tropics some hosts (e.g. weavers) build hanging nests with entrances too small for a cuckoo to enter, and with long funnels leading to the egg-chamber. It would seem impossible for a cuckoo to enter the nest to lay directly, or to project an egg in from the entrance, yet tropical cuckoos still manage to victimize such hosts. Maybe they insert the egg directly through the nest material; the damage so caused being repaired by the male host who probably built the main structure unaided by his mate.

Parasitism can be a threat, therefore, no matter how well concealed or constructed the nest. Colonial nesting is also no sure defence, and could even make laying by the parasite easier. Some female tropical cuckoos (e.g. Didric) limit their egg-laying to one group of nests in a single tree. Because of the abundance of nests, the cuckoo does not need to watch each one closely in order to lay at the right time, but can inspect a number of nests on each laying day and quickly find one at a suitable stage. Most cuckoos, and other brood parasites, apparently locate the nests of their hosts by watching them building. The onset of nest building by the host is thought to stimulate ovulation in the female parasite, which means that her egg can be laid when the host is also laying, an important strategy if the resulting young parasite is to hatch no later than its foster siblings.

Most parasitic cuckoos victimize hosts smaller than themselves. As discussed earlier (Chapter 1), some may be hawk-mimetic and possibly frighten away their hosts when laying. In others, which parasitize larger hosts, there is some evidence that the male helps the female by luring the host pair away from their nest. In all cases, however, the female is quiet and unobtrusive, slipping in to lay at an opportune moment when the hosts are not looking. Mostly female cuckoos are cryptically coloured to avoid detection. When mobbed by small birds, European Cuckoos have no defence other than to fly off and hide. Exceptionally a Cuckoo will expose its red gape to a mobbing bird: Benson (1959) even saw a Dunnock feed an adult Cuckoo that did this. If physically attacked when trying to lay, female Cuckoos are not often deterred from their mission. They are usually successful despite the host's attempts to stop them. I once saw about eight Sedge Warblers attacking a female Cuckoo laying in a Reed Warbler nest about 2m away from a Sedge Warbler nest containing small young. Several individuals took turns at clinging to the Cuckoo and pulling out feathers from its head and neck (colour plate 13). The Cuckoo took no notice, laid her egg, and flew off with the Sedge Warblers in hot pursuit. All this time, one of the Reed Warblers was singing in the background.

The effects of aggression are minimized by having the egg ready to be laid in the oviduct, so that the actual placing of the egg into the nest need take no more than a few seconds (see Chapter 8). The female Cuckoo also removes one or more of the host's eggs when laying her own. This has the effect of not increasing the clutch size beyond the incubating capacity of the host, and may also help to confuse the host by simulating an egg-robber, and reduce aggression towards the parasite's egg. The host, even when trying to stop a laying Cuckoo, only sees the Cuckoo remove one of its eggs, it does not see the Cuckoo lay its own egg.

The shell of a Cuckoo's egg is thicker than the host's: this may protect it when laid, and possibly prevents some hosts breaking the egg. If they cannot break it, they may be unable to remove it from the nest. Possibly, the harder Cuckoo egg may break some of the host's eggs if projected into a nest carelessly: this could cause more frequent desertion in species such as the Wren (see Table 15).

Despite the above adaptations by cuckoos to counter host defences and because desertion and discrimination are the best forms of defence, the most significant development is undoubtedly that of egg-mimicry. The eggs of many parasitic cuckoos match perfectly, or nearly so, those of their respective hosts in size, colour and markings. The hosts themselves are thought to have been largely responsible for producing this mimetic resemblance. Through their powers of egg-recognition they have continually rejected ill-matched eggs and accepted only those which looked like their own. As the hosts' eggs evolved colours and patterns to avoid detection by predators, parasitic cuckoo eggs evolved similar colours to avoid rejection by the hosts. Old notions that different diets produced different coloured eggs in cuckoos, or that a cuckoo 'chose' a host with similar coloured eggs to its own, have now been discarded. The subject was first extensively researched by Baker (1942) and is discussed here in more detail in Chapter 9.

When they hatch in the host's nests of course, young cuckoos also possess some adaptations to improve their survival. The overwhelming psychological stimulus of a gaping and calling youngster in the nest is probably enough to ensure that the hosts bring food and feed the cuckoo. Young European Cuckoos have a bright orange-red mouth lining which seems to act as a 'super-stimulus' to the hosts, most, if not all, of whose own young, depending on species, have orange, red or yellow gapes. Exaggerated food-begging calls may also ensure that the hosts do not desert. The importance of these features is illustrated by the fact that other birds, beside the actual host pair, will feed a young Cuckoo. Even young songbirds, especially flycatchers, that were barely able to feed themselves fed a young Cuckoo brought into captivity with them (Sokolowski 1958).

Because they eject their foster siblings from the nest soon after hatching, most young cuckoos preclude the possibility that the foster parents might selectively feed only their rightful offspring. However, in cuckoo species in which the young are reared alongside their host's young (e.g. Koel), the young cuckoos are thought to resemble the host young (Jourdain 1925). There is obviously scope here for experimentally testing the effect of mimicry and the ability of the host to discriminate. In another group of brood parasites, the widowbirds of Africa, nestling mimicry has evolved to a very advanced stage. Each species of widowbird parasitizes only one species of estrildine finch, the young of which have special mouth markings unique to the species. The young widowbirds are raised with the host young and have identical mouth markings, calls and food-begging postures (Nicolai 1974).

Effects of parasitism on hosts

No matter how the hosts try to hide or defend their nests, therefore, parasitic birds have often found some counter-measure. Many potential host species (e.g. *Phylloscopus* warblers against the Cuckoo) are relatively free from brood parasites because they have rigorously defended against them. Others have not been so successful. While it is in most cases disadvantageous to the individual to be parasitized, in one case it even seems to be beneficial. In Central America, Smith (1968) found that the Giant Cowbird, *Scaphidura oryzivora* almost exclusively parasitized other colonial Icterids (oropendolas and caciques). In a complex system of host-parasite relationships he found that a colony of hosts nesting alongside bees or wasps produced more young than colonies away from bees where heavy nestling mortality was caused by botfly infestation. Colonies nesting away from bees or wasps that were parasitized by Giant Cowbirds lost only 8.4 per cent of their offspring through botflies, compared to 90 per cent mortality from botflies in colonies without the bees or the cowbirds. In other words, it was an advantage to be parasitized if there were no bees. This was because the young cowbirds preened the host young ridding them of botfly larvae, something the host young could not do for themselves. In this system the hosts could also be separated into rejectors and non-rejectors of cowbird eggs on a colonial basis: all the individuals of one colony reacted in the same way. In the rejecting colonies there was accurate egg-mimicry by the cowbirds, whereas in the non-rejecting colonies there was not. The non-discriminating hosts nested earlier in the season and benefited from cowbird parasitism by reduced botfly infestation of their chicks, but the later nesting colonies, which were protected from botflies by bees or wasps, discriminated against cowbird eggs resulting in mimetic eggs. This implied two genetically distinct types of cowbird parasitizing the same host species.

Cowbirds, widowbirds and some cuckoos have young which are reared with the host young and, therefore, do not prevent production of young by their hosts – they only reduce it. Similarly, the Black-headed Duck does not prevent production of young by its hosts. The majority of young parasitic cuckoos and honeyguides, on the other hand, are reared to the exclusion of the host young because they either eject, kill or smother them. Nevertheless, this does not preclude the hosts rearing a brood of their own at another time in the season.

Since parasitic birds are relatively scarce in the environment and they victimize mainly common species, the overall effects of parasitism on host populations are small. Using only results by workers who recorded all the nests of hosts throughout their breeding season in particular areas, Table 17 shows that some potential hosts may be almost completely neglected while others may suffer more than 50 per cent parasitism at the local level. A high frequency of parasitism in cuckoo species which destroy all the host young tends to occur only in small study areas (e.g. G. Schiermann in Lack 1963, working on a small colony of Reed Warblers near Berlin). Most examples in Table 17 (20 out of 26) were below 20 per cent parasitism. In cuckoo species where the young grow up together with the host young, the frequency of parasitism was generally much higher (10 out of 12 examples over 20 per cent).

One advantage of not destroying the host young and having a higher parasitism frequency is that the parasites can lay more than one egg in each nest, whereas the young-ejectors have to lay singly into a lot of different nests. The ejector-species then have to rely on abundant hosts, while the non-ejectors can also exploit scarcer species.

Parasitism frequencies on a local scale are not the same as those on host populations over large regions. Glue and Morgan (1972) examined the British Trust for Ornithology's nest record cards for the years 1939–1971 and found that parasitism by British Cuckoos barely exceeded 3 per cent of any host species. A study of nest record cards in southern Africa by Payne and Payne (1967) revealed that 66 host species were parasitized by nine species of cuckoos. Four host species suffered more than 10 per cent parasitism, mainly by species of *Clamator* cuckoos which do not eject the host young. Ten host species, including four more hosts of *Clamators* suffered 3–10 per cent parasitism, but the majority (52) had less than 3 per cent of their nests parasitized by cuckoos. In comparison, 15 host species of Brown-headed Cowbirds, *Molothrus ater* in Ontario, Canada were parasitized at rates of 0.2–33.3 per cent (Robertson and Norman 1976). In a later work, Payne (1977) tabulated the effect of various brood parasites on the fledging success of some hosts and calculated that the reduction in recruitment to host populations was generally below 20 per cent even at the local level.

Hosts of *Cuculus canorus*

With such an extensive breeding range from north-west Europe to Japan, the Common Cuckoo has been found to parasitize a large number of birds. More than 125 species have been recorded as hosts, with a total of nearly 100 in Europe alone (Table 18). In fact, only 11 host species in Europe are parasitized frequently and about the same number occasionally. The latter appear to be used mainly when an individual Cuckoo has exhausted the local supply of its usual hosts (e.g. Reed Warbler-Cuckoos sometimes lay eggs in nests of nearby Sedge Warblers), or perhaps when an individual bird is 'geared' to parasitizing an unusual host species which it may have been reared by, or lastly, where a particular host species forms the most abundant local passerine (e.g. Rock Pipits on British coasts). The parasitism frequency of the most common host species varies from region to region, giving an irregular pattern of host-use in Europe. In Britain the main host species are Meadow Pipit, Dunnock and Reed Warbler. The same holds for the Netherlands, Belgium and northern France. However, in central Europe the main host is the Garden Warbler, with Meadow Pipit, White Wagtail, Robin and others in different regions. In Czechoslovakia, the Robin and Redstart are the usual main hosts.

Such is the complexity of host-use in Europe that there are relatively few regions where only one species forms the main Cuckoo host. Notable among these are Finland and Sweden, where Bramblings (in the north) and Redstarts (in the centre) are the principal hosts, and in Hungary, where the Great Reed Warbler is the main victim in the extensive reedbeds and marshes. In these regions Cuckoos have consistently parasitized only one main host, resulting in the evolution, through host-discrimination and natural selection, of near-perfect mimetic eggs. Elsewhere, especially in central and north-west Europe, egg-mimicry is generally poorer, probably because the Cuckoos have not concentrated on one main host species (see Chapter 9).

Outside central and north-west Europe, host-selection by Cuckoos follows a similar pattern. In any region there may be only one or two principal hosts, but a great number of occasional and rare ones. In central Russia Tree Pipit, Robin and White Wagtail are still the main hosts, but further east in central Asia main hosts include a reed thrush and species of chat. East of the Caspian Sea it is the Streaked Scrub Warbler, *Scotocerca inquieta*, but in the far north-east of Russia (Amur), a species of shrike and Thick-billed Reed Warbler, *Acrocephalus aedon* form the main hosts (Dement'ev *et al* 1966).

The southern and middle Asian race *subtelephonus* chiefly foists its

Table 17 *Parasitism rates on local host populations*

Parasite	Host	Region	No. nests	No. parasitized	%	Source
(a) Parasites raised alone						
European Cuckoo, *Cuculus canorus*	Tree Pipit, *Anthus trivialis*	NE England	85	6	7	Lack 1963 (A. Whitaker)
	Meadow Pipit, *A. pratensis*	NE England	77	7	9	Lack 1963 (A. Whitaker)
	Pied Wagtail, *Motacilla alba*	NE England	74	2	3	Lack 1963 (A. Whitaker)
		Derbyshire	34	3	9	Lack 1963 (F. C. R. Jourdain)
	Dunnock, *Prunella modularis*	NE England	357	7	2	Lack 1963 (A. Whitaker)
		Derbyshire	66	1	1	Lack 1963 (F.C.R.J.)
		Berkshire	49	9	18	Lack 1963 (F.C.R.J.)
		Berkshire/Oxfordshire	244	12	5	Lack 1963 (H. Mayer-Gross)
	Reed Warbler, *Acrocephalus scirpaceus*	Nottinghamshire	232	45	19	Lack 1963 (A. Whitaker)
		Berlin, Germany	78	43	55	Lack 1963 (G. Schiermann)
		Munich, Germany	177	16	9	Lack 1963 (G. Diesselhorst)
		Alsace, France	1,099	235	21	Blaise 1965
		Cambridgeshire	1,367	170	12	present study
	Great Reed Warbler, *A. arundinaceus*	Sarvos, Hungary	374	189	50	Molnar 1944
	Sedge Warbler, *A. schoenobaernus*	NE England	89	8	9	Lack 1963 (A. Whitaker)
	Robin, *Erithacus*	Derbyshire	135	1	1	Lack 1963 (F.C.R.J.)

Parasite	Host young	Locality				Reference
catcher, *Batis pririt* / Yellow-bellied Bush Warbler, *Eremomela icteropygialis*		SW Africa	7	2	29	Jensen & Clinning 1975
Didric Cuckoo, *Chrysococcyx caprius*	Masked Weaver, *Ploceus vellatus*	Transvaal	120	12	10	Hunter 1961
			38	7	18	Friedmann 1949
	Red Bishop, *Euplectes orix*	Natal	749	72	10	Jensen & Vernon 1970
		Transvaal	52	13	25	Reed 1968
Black Cuckoo, *Cuculus clamosus*	Crimson-breasted Shrike, *Laniarius atrococcineus*	SW Africa	28	10	36	Jensen & Clinning 1975

(b) Parasites raised with host young

Parasite	Host young	Locality				Reference
Great Spotted Cuckoo, *Clamator glandarius*	Magpie, *Pica pica*	Spain	50	8	16	Mountfort 1958
			20	5	25	Valverde 1971
	Pied Crow, *Corvus albus*	Nigeria	23	5	22	Mundy & Cooke 1977
Jacobin Cuckoo, *Clamator jacobinus*	Cape Bulbul, *Pycnonotus capensis*	South Africa	115	41	36	Liversidge 1971
Koel, *Eudynamis scolopacea*	House Crow, *Corvus splendens*	India	20	3	15	Lamba 1963
Giant Cowbird, *Scaphidura oryzivora*	Oropendolas (3 species) & caciques (1 species)	Panama	1,993 (no botfly)	567	28	Smith 1968
			1,277 (+ botfly)	935	73	Smith 1968
Shiny Cowbird, *Molothrus bonariensis*	Rufous-collared Sparrow, *Zonotrichia capensis*	Buenos Aires, Argentina	45	31	69	Fraga 1978
Brown-headed Cowbird, *Molothrus ater*	Eastern Phoebe, *Sayornis phoebe*	Kansas, USA	391	95	24	Klaas 1975
Indigo-Bird, *Vidua chalybeata*	Red-billed Firefinch, *Lagonosticta senegala*	Senegal	374	133	36	Morel 1973
		Zambia	31	13	42	Payne 1977
Black-headed Duck, *Heteronetta atricapilla*	Red-fronted Coot, *Fulica rufifrons*	Buenos Aires, Argentina	133	73	55	Weller 1968

eggs on Great Reed Warblers. The Japanese *telephonus* uses three main hosts with 16 occasional or rare ones. In Algeria, the southern *bangsi* race parasitizes Moussier's Redstart, but in Europe Whitethroat and Sardinian Warbler. In Assam, northern India, Baker (1942) recorded 103 hosts of the race *bakeri* which parasitized only 23 regularly.

Successful hosts of European Cuckoos (Table 18) range in size from Goldcrests weighing a mere 5.5g to Blackbirds at about 90g, only 20g less than the adult Cuckoo weight. However, hosts at these extremes are only rarely parasitized and most regular hosts weigh in the range 10–25g, or about 15 per cent of the Cuckoo weight. In fact, a young Cuckoo reaches this weight at only three or four days old. Nearly all hosts are insectivorous species or species which feed their young initially on insects. Young Cuckoos are rarely, if ever, successfully raised by non-insectivorous hosts.

Hosts of other parasitic cuckoos

The total numbers of recorded host species for some other parasitic cuckoos are listed in Table 19. Most cuckoos, it would seem, regularly parasitize only one or two species, but their eggs or young have been found either occasionally or rarely in the nests of many others. In Africa, for example, the Red-chested Cuckoo, *Cuculus solitarius*, has 45 recorded host species yet concentrates on only two – the Cape Wagtail, *Motacilla capensis* and Robin-Chat, *Cossypha caffra* – while the Black Cuckoo, *Cuculus clamosus*, has 19 recorded hosts, but uses mainly shrikes, *Laniarius*. The Striped Crested Cuckoo, *Clamator levaillanti*, in Africa parasitizes mainly the Arrow-marked Babbler, *Turdoides jardinei*, while its relative the African Jacobin Cuckoo, *C. jacobinus* uses two species of bulbuls, *Pycnonotus*. The glossy cuckoos (*Chrysococcyx*) in Africa also specialize on different main hosts: the Didric on weavers, the Emerald on bulbuls, and Klaas Cuckoo on sunbirds and warblers. In Japan there are four species of cuckoo in the same genus (*Cuculus*) each parasitic on different main hosts (see Table 19).

All parasitic cuckoos, except the Cuckoo in most of Europe, live in the same area as one or more of their parasitic relatives. Host-specialization is one way to avoid competition between different cuckoo species in the same area. If, for example, the four Japanese cuckoos all parasitized the same common host, they would each harm the others by (i) depletion of the particular host population, and (ii) by ejection of each other's eggs by the young. Friedmann (1964) proposed a model of the evolutionary history of the crested *Clamator* cuckoos based on their present-day host selection, egg colours and plumages. He suggested that the group started

Table 18 *Species parasitized by the Cuckoo, Cuculus canorus, in Europe*

Group of host species	Status as hosts	Main region	Degree of egg-mimicry
Tree Pipit, *Anthus trivialis**	F	Russia, Poland	Generally good
Meadow Pipit, *Anthus pratensis**	F	Britain, France, Germany, Poland, Norway	
Rock Pipit, *Anthus spinoletta**	O	Britain, France?	
Tawny Pipit, *Anthus campestris*	R		
White/Pied Wagtail, *Motacilla alba**	F	Britain, Netherlands, Germany, Poland, southern Scandinavia, Russia	Generally good
Grey Wagtail, *Motacilla cinerea**	R		
Yellow Wagtail, *Motacilla flava*	O	Netherlands	
Dunnock, *Prunella modularis**	F	Britain, France, Netherlands, Switzerland, Germany	None
Alpine Accentor, *Prunella collaris*	R		
Reed Warbler, *Acrocephalus scirpaceus**	F	Britain, France, Netherlands, Germany	Generally good
Great Reed Warbler, *Acrocephalus arundinaceus**	F	Hungary, Russia	
Marsh Warbler, *Acrocephalus palustris**	O	Hungary, Germany, Netherlands	
Sedge Warbler, *Acrocephalus schoenobaenus*	O	Britain, Netherlands, northern Germany, Poland	
Whitethroat, *Sylvia communis**	O	Southern countries	Generally good
Lesser Whitethroat, *Sylvia curruca*	R		
Garden Warbler, *Sylvia borin**	F	Germany, Poland, central countries	
Blackcap, *Sylvia atricapilla*	O	Central countries	
Sardinian Warbler, *Sylvia melanocephala*	R?	Southern countries?	
Orphean Warbler, *Sylvia hortensis*	R?		
Dartford Warbler, *Sylvia undata*	R?		
Barred Warbler, *Sylvia nisoria*	R?		

contd.

Table 18   contd.

Group of host species	Status as hosts	Main region	Degree of egg-mimicry
Willow Warbler, *Phylloscopus trochilus*	R		
Wood Warbler, *Phylloscopus sibilatrix**	R		
Chiffchaff, *Phylloscopus collybita*	R	Throughout central and northern countries	Poor
Icterine Warbler, *Hippolais icterina*	R		
Grasshopper Warbler, *Locustella naevia*	R		
Spotted Flycatcher, *Muscicapa striata**	R		
Swallow, *Hirundo rustica**	R	Throughout central and northern countries	Poor
Goldcrest, *Regulus regulus*	R		
Wren, *Troglodytes troglodytes**	O		
Woodlark, *Lullula arborea*	R	As pipits	Fair
Skylark, *Alauda arvensis*	O		
Robin, *Erithacus rubecula**	F	Germany, Czechoslovakia, Russia	Good
Redstart, *Phoenicurus phoenicurus**	F	Scandinavia, Russia, Czechoslovakia, Germany	
Black Redstart, *Phoenicurus ochrurus*	R		
Pied Flycatcher, *Ficedula hypoleuca*	R		
Stonechat, *Saxicola torquata**	O	Central and north-eastern countries	Excellent
Whinchat, *Saxicola rubetra*	R		
Wheatear, *Oenanthe oenanthe*	R		
Nightingale, *Luscinia megarhynchos*	R		
Blackbird, *Turdus merula**	R	Throughout central and northern countries	None

Brambling, Fringilla montifringilla*	F	Northern Scandinavia, Russia	Good
Chaffinch, Fringilla coelebs	O	Finland, Russia	
Greenfinch, Carduelis chloris	R		
Linnet, Acanthis cannabina	O	Britain, Netherlands, Germany	
Goldfinch, Carduelis carduelis	R		
Bullfinch, Pyrrhula pyrrhula	R		None
Hawfinch, Coccothraustes coccothraustes	R		
Redpoll, Acanthis flammea	R		
Twite, Acanthis flavirostris	R		
Yellowhammer, Emberiza citrinella	O	Britain, Netherlands, Germany	
Reed Bunting, Emberiza schoeniculus*	O	Britain, Netherlands, Germany	Poor

F = frequent; O = occasional; R = rare or accidental
* Known to have reared a young Cuckoo

Cuckoo eggs are also said to have been found in nests of the following species:

Shore Lark (Eremophila alpestris), Short-toed Lark (Calandrella cinerea), Crested Lark (Galerida cristata), Red-throated Pipit (Anthus cervinus), Richard's Pipit (Anthus novaeseelandiae), Lesser Grey Shrike (Lanius minor), Woodchat Shrike (Lanius senator), Aquatic Warbler (Acrocephalus paludicola), Firecrest (Regulus ignicapillus), Rock Thrush (Monticola saxatilis), Bluethroat (Luscinia svecica), Thrush-nightingale (Luscinia luscinia), Bearded Tit (Panurus biarmicus), Long-tailed Tit (Aegithelos caudatus), Great Tit (Parus major), Treecreeper (Certhia familiaris), Short-toed Treecreeper (Certhia brachydactyla), Corn Bunting (Emberiza calandra), Cirl Bunting (Emberiza cirlus), Ortolan Bunting (Emberiza hortulana), Rustic Bunting (Emberiza rustica), Lapland Bunting (Calcarius lapponicus), Serin (Serinus serinus), Tree Sparrow (Passer montanus), House Sparrow (Passer domesticus), Starling (Sturnus vulgaris), Golden Oriole (Oriolus oriolus).

Instances of Cuckoo eggs being found in the nests of the following species have been recorded, but seem unlikely to be correct:
Little Grebe (Tachybaptus ruficollis), Pheasant (Phasianus colchicus), Greenshank (Tringa nebularia), Woodpigeon (Columba palumbus), Stock Dove (Columba oenas), Turtle Dove (Streptopelia turta), Fieldfare (Turdus pilaris), Redwing (Turdus iliacus), Mistle Thrush (Turdus viscivorus), Dipper (Cinclus cinclus), Jay (Garrulus glandarius), Magpie (Pica pica), Jackdaw (Corvus monedula).

Table 19 *Numbers and main host species of some other parasitic cuckoos*

Cuckoo	Region	No. of main host species	Main hosts	Occasional	Rare	Total	Main source
Oriental Cuckoo, *Cuculus saturatus*	Himalayas	1	Blyth's Crowned Willow Warbler, *Phylloscopus reguloides*	4	11	16	Baker 1942
	Japan	1	Crowned Willow Warbler, *Phylloscopus occipitalis*	(13)		14	Royama 1963
Large Hawk-Cuckoo, *Cuculus sparverioides*	Asia	1	Streaked Spider Hunter, *Arachnothera magna*	6	21	28	Baker 1942
Fugitive Hawk-Cuckoo, *Cuculus fugax*	Japan	4	Red-flanked Bluetail, *Luscinia cyanurus*; Japanese Robin, *L. akahige*; Blue Robin, *L. cyane*; Blue Flycatcher, *Muscicapa cyanomelana*	(6)		10	Royama 1963
	India	1	Small Niltava, *Niltava macgrigoriae*	3	16	20	Baker 1942
Common Hawk-Cuckoo, *Cuculus varius*	India	1	Jungle Babbler, *Turdoides striatus*	4	12	17	Baker 1942
Short-winged Cuckoo, *Cuculus micropterus*	India	1	Streaked Laughingthrush, *Garrulax lineatus*	–	10	11	Baker 1942
Lesser Cuckoo, *Cuculus poliocephalus*	Asia (including Japan)	1	Strong-footed Bush Warbler, *Cettia forticeps*	8	13	22	Baker 1942
	Japan	2	Wren, *Troglodytes troglodytes* Bush Warbler, *Cettia diphone*	(5)		7	Royama 1963
Black Cuckoo, *Cuculus clamosus*	Africa	1	Southern Boubou Shrike, *Laniarius ferrugineus*	4	14	19	Friedmann 1967
							Payne & Payne 1967
Red-chested Cuckoo, *Cuculus solitarius*	Africa	2	Cape Wagtail, *Motacilla capensis*; Robin-Chat, *Cossypha caffra*	7	36	45	Friedmann 1967
Plaintive Cuckoo, *Cacomantis merulinus*	Burma	1	Fantail Warbler, *Cisticola juncidis*	6	7	14	Baker 1942
	India	1	Ashy Long-tailed Warbler, *Prinia socialis*	4	3	8	Baker 1942
Banded Bay Cuckoo,	Asia	1	White-eyed Quaker Babbler,				

Cuckoo species	Region		Principal hosts				Reference
Horsfield's Bronze Cuckoo, *Chrysococcyx basalis*	Australia	1	Superb Wren-Warbler, *Malurus cyaneus*	12	87	100	Friedmann 1968
Shining Bronze Cuckoo, *Chrysococcyx lucidus*	Australia, New Zealand	2	Grey Warbler, *Gerygone igata*. Yellow-tailed Thornbill, *Acanthiza chrysorrhoa*	11	71	84	Friedmann 1968
Black-eared Cuckoo, *Chrysococcyx osculans*	Australia	1	Speckled Warbler, *Chthonicola sagittata*	1	9	11	Friedmann 1968
Didric Cuckoo, *Chrysococcyx caprius*	Africa	2	Masked Weaver, *Ploceus velatus*; Red Bishop, *Euplectes orix*	15	50	67	Friedmann 1968
African Emerald Cuckoo, *Chrysococcyx cupreus*	Africa	1	Common Bulbul, *Pycnonotus barbatus*	7	26	34	Friedmann 1968
Klaas Cuckoo, *Chrysococcyx klaas*	Africa	3	Scarlet-chested Sunbird, *Nectarinia senegalensis*; Red-chested Sunbird, *N. erythroceria*; Tawny Prinia, *Prinia subflava*	12	44	59	Friedmann 1968
Red-winged Crested Cuckoo, *Clamator coromondus*	Asia	1	Lesser Necklaced Laughing-thrush, *Garrulax moniligera*	10	14	25	Friedmann 1964; Baker 1942
Great Spotted Cuckoo, *Clamator glandarius*	Europe—Africa	3	Magpie, *Pica pica*; Pied Crow, *Corvus albus*; Black Crow, *Corvus capensis*	6	13	22	Friedmann 1964
Striped Crested Cuckoo, *Clamator levaillanti*	Africa	1	Arrow-marked Babbler, *Turdoides jardinei*	(10)		11	Friedmann 1964; Payne & Payne 1967
Jacobin Cuckoo, *Clamator jacobinus*	Asia	1	Lesser Necklaced Laughing-thrush, *Garrulax moniligera*	10	23	34	Baker 1942
	Africa	2	Common Bulbul, *Pycnonotus barbatus*; Cape Bulbul, *Pycnonotus capensis*	5	9	16	Friedmann 1964
Koel, *Eudynamis scolopacea*	Asia—Australia	1	House Crow, *Corvus splendens*	3	8	12	Baker 1942

Figures in parentheses are numbers of occasional and rare hosts combined.

in southern Africa with *C. jacobinus* because this species lays white, non-mimetic eggs in the nests of bulbuls. An evolutionary offshoot, *C. levaillanti*, developed in southern Africa and began parasitizing babblers to avoid competition. *C. jacobinus*, Friedmann proposed, then spread northward in Africa and possibly began parasitizing babblers where it met no competition from *C. levaillanti*. When it reached Asia, *C. jacobinus* concentrated on babblers, free from any competition, and developed a high degree of egg-mimicry. Next, *C. coromondus* developed in Asia and parasitized laughingthrushes, again avoiding competition and again developing good egg-mimicry with the hosts. Finally, *C. glandarius* developed and spread westward into Europe where it found Magpies, *Pica pica*, suitable hosts and developed a high degree of mimicry of their eggs. This last species then spread into North Africa where it parasitized crows, and probably recently into southern Africa where it now also parasitizes glossy starlings.

This model illustrates how competition for suitable hosts by parasitic cuckoos may have influenced their evolutionary development and spread into new areas. Today's cuckoos, although mostly living in the same areas as one another, avoid competition by exploiting, for the most part, different hosts.

8 | Egg-laying

The method by which the egg of a parasitic cuckoo is introduced into the host nest has long aroused controversy and speculation. The discovery of cuckoo eggs in seemingly inaccessible nests, where it was regarded as impossible for a cuckoo to lay directly, gave rise to alternative suggestions for egg-deposition. These were thoroughly discussed by Chance (1940) in respect of the European Cuckoo, and by Baker (1942) for Asiatic cuckoo species. Chance witnessed over 100 layings by European Cuckoos in Meadow Pipit nests, and refused to believe that any method was used other than the one he always saw: that of direct laying by sitting on the nest. But in India, where there are several parasitic cuckoo species parasitizing a wider range of nest-types, Baker was less certain, and thought that the egg was in some cases introduced by the bill.

Methods of egg-deposition

Despite the wide range of host species used by parasitic cuckoos, most of them build open, cup-shaped nests concealed in vegetation. The European Cuckoo can experience little difficulty in laying directly into the nests of most of its main host species, and all observations so far indicate that direct laying by squatting on the nest is the only method used. Colour plates 3 and 6 show female Cuckoos laying directly into the open nests of Reed Warblers.

A second category of host includes the niche- or hole-nesters such as wagtails, flycatchers, redstarts, robins, etc. To these may be added the dome-nesters – wrens and some warblers. In most instances it is doubtful whether a Cuckoo could sit on such nests to lay an egg directly. It is generally believed that the egg is projected into the nest by pressing the cloaca as near to the entrance as possible and 'squirting' the egg in. To do this the Cuckoo has to cling to the nest (in the case of Wrens), or to the surrounding structure in which the nest is built. The thick shell of a Cuckoo's egg protects it when dropped into a nest, although some of the host's eggs may be damaged. (It is possible that such breakage causes more frequent desertion by hosts with these nest-types, as discussed in the last chapter).

In the European Cuckoo, direct laying is the only reliably reported method, while the projection method may be used when the clutch is less accessible. Nevertheless, there are other ways that a parasitic cuckoo might introduce its egg into the host nest. Earlier this century, the near universal belief was that the egg was laid on the ground, picked up in the cuckoo's bill, and carried to the nest. This allegedly gave the cuckoo the chance to examine its egg and 'choose' a nest containing similarly coloured eggs. A slight variation of this tale was for the cuckoo to carry its egg in its throat, and 'regurgitate' it into the appropriate nest. Edgar Chance discredited all reported instances of such behaviour, claiming that in most cases the observer saw the cuckoo carrying one of the host's eggs, not its own. Baker (1942), on the other hand, thought that egg-placement by the bill was an occasional practice in some Asiatic cuckoos. For example, he cited the Indian Plaintive Cuckoo, *Cacomantis merulinus* parasitizing the warblers *Cistocola juncidis* and *Franklinia gracilis*. These tiny and common hosts build nests cleverly sewn into leaves which 'under no possible circumstances' could the Plaintive Cuckoo enter to lay. Furthermore, they are built in such sites as to afford a cuckoo no foothold if it tried to project an egg through the entrance. Yet Baker and his colleagues found these nests regularly and successfully parasitized, the nests and eggs being quite undamaged. In 1907 the Plaintive Cuckoo was particularly abundant in Baker's study area, so he instructed his assistants to set nooses at the entrance of nearly 300 nests of the Fantail Warbler. They caught three female Plaintive Cuckoos, each by the neck, and each nest contained a cuckoo's egg. The inference was that they became caught when withdrawing their heads having put an egg into the nest. Baker pointed out that the cuckoos could have first projected their eggs into the nests and became caught when trying to remove one of the host's eggs, but he thought this an unlikely tactic because of the risk of the cuckoo removing its own egg. He also mentioned the possibility that a cuckoo might hover in front of a nest-entrance to put an egg in with its bill, but produced no evidence for this.

Another possibility mentioned in the last chapter is mainly applicable to tropical cuckoos. In some passerine hosts, the male builds the nest and the female merely lines it before laying. Sometimes the female starts laying before the nest is complete, and if a cuckoo did the same, any damage caused could be repaired by the male of the host pair. A seemingly inaccessible clutch could then be successfully parasitized.

At present, there is no conclusive evidence, as far as I am aware, for egg-deposition by the bill in any species of cuckoo; but the inference of its occurrence remains high. A detailed study, like that by Edgar Chance, of a cuckoo parasitic on a host species that builds in a difficult site could provide the evidence required.

The laying procedure

Egg-laying by European Cuckoos has been observed many times, mainly by Edgar Chance, and is now a well-documented event. Irrespective of host species or region, the behaviour seems to be the same, with only slight individual variations. Unaided by a male, the female Cuckoo first seeks out her particular host species and locates their nests by watching them building. To find the nests she is prepared to spend several hours each day without feeding or revealing herself. Occasionally she may visit a nest-site a few days, or even hours, before laying, presumably to check the location or stage of development. The hawk-like gliding flight is used during such pre-laying nest visits. I once watched a female Cuckoo attempting to lay in a Meadow Pipit nest which was about 100m from the nearest tree. The Cuckoo was first spotted gliding around a 40-hectare meadow at mid-morning on 23 June. She made repeated stops either on the ground or on tufts of coarse grass, or in the large tree on the edge of the field. On the ground she disappeared into the grass and appeared to be searching hurriedly through it. There were three or four pairs of pipits occasionally in attendance, but their intensity of attack seemed no greater when the Cuckoo was near their nests than elsewhere. After seven hours of this (by now it was evening), she eventually found the nest, laid her egg and flew off carrying one of the pipit's eggs. It might have taken a man with a trained dog as long to have found this nest: I only found it after I had seen the Cuckoo fly off with the stolen egg.

Normally, however, and especially when parasitizing Reed Warblers, a female Cuckoo takes up a hidden position much nearer the nest, usually less than 50m away. She adopts a horizontal position, lying along a branch in the manner of a Nightjar, *Caprimulgus europaeus*. This further reduces her conspicuousness, but even discovery by the hosts at this stage does not perturb a Cuckoo intent on laying. Several hours may be spent in this position, allowing the egg to pass along the oviduct ready for immediate extrusion when she arrives at the nest. Perhaps some eggs are wasted during this process because they are laid prematurely: Dr A. G. Butler, cited by Baker (1942), saw a Cuckoo settle on a bar of a gate and lay an egg – he was so excited that instead of waiting to see if the Cuckoo picked it up to take it to a suitable nest, as Baker thought it might, he rushed up to claim the intact egg.

With an egg in the oviduct ready for laying, the female Cuckoo glides like a hawk to the nest-site, landing either directly on the nest or in the vegetation nearby. As a rule, she will not know the nest's exact position within a few square metres, and probably finds it by searching the area. On reaching the nest she clings to the rim with her zygodactyl feet and balances with outstretched wings and tail. The feet remain at the back of the nest and do not enter the cup where they might damage the eggs. Invariably one of the host's eggs is picked up in the bill and held while the Cuckoo raises her abdomen over the rim of the nest to bring her cloaca over the clutch. The egg is then extruded with a shudder. The Cuckoo flies off immediately without looking at her egg, and still carrying the robbed host's egg which is swallowed whole or crushed and eaten. Occasionally one or more eggs are eaten in quick succession while the Cuckoo is at the nest, but always before she has laid her own; if she took an egg after laying, as reported by Joy (1943), there would be a risk of eating her own. For 83 instances in Reed Warbler nests in Cambridgeshire where the number of eggs removed by a laying Cuckoo was known, 74 (89 per cent) involved one or two eggs, while only four nests had three eggs taken (Table 20). Only rarely were no eggs taken by a laying female, but this usually in nests that were empty anyway. In fact, these data largely reflect the number of eggs in the nest on the laying day as shown in Table 21, illustrating the close synchronism between the laying of the Cuckoo and that of the host. Some individual females parasitizing Reed Warblers were more prone to take more than one egg than others, and one bird in particular at my study site usually ate all the eggs present.

The time taken to lay the egg is remarkably swift. From the moment the Cuckoo arrives at the nest until she leaves with one of the host's eggs having laid her own, can take as little as three or four seconds. Edgar Chance found the average laying time to be less that ten seconds in Meadow Pipit nests, and Molnar (1944) recorded a duration of eight

Table 20 *Number of host eggs removed by Cuckoos laying in Reed Warbler nests, Cambs. 1974–1979*

	Number of eggs taken						
	0	1	2	3	4	5	Total
Number of instances	5	51	23	4			83
Number of females	4	16	8	2			

Table 21 *Number of eggs in host nest when parasitized by Cuckoos*

| | Number of eggs present | | | | | | |
	0	1	2	3	4	5	Total
Number of Meadow Pipit nests (Chance 1940)	4	17	20	14	13	4	72
Number of Reed Warbler nests (Cambs. 1974–79)	4	25	33	21	6	1	90
Total	8	42	53	35	19	5	162

seconds in nests of Great Reed Warblers. Compared to these two species, Reed Warblers are non-aggressive towards a laying Cuckoo, yet Cuckoos I have watched in Cambridgeshire usually laid in less than 10 seconds. Occasionally a female Cuckoo remained on the nest for over a minute and it was during these instances that more than one egg was eaten. In general, though, rapid egg-laying minimizes the chance of detection by the hosts and further reduces aggression by them towards the Cuckoo and its egg. It also reduces the possibility of attracting predators or rival females to the host nest.

Most small bird species, including hosts of the Cuckoo, lay each egg on consecutive days in the early morning. Reed Warblers, for example, lay mainly around sunrise. Cuckoos lay much later in the day – usually in the late afternoon or early evening. Table 22 gives the egg-laying times for a number of female Cuckoos using different host species. There is a slight bias since the birds were often delayed by their observers, but only two out of 120 cases were before noon; one only two minutes before, the other at 0940 hours BST. (The latter was Chance's Cuckoo A's last egg of the 1921 season and was not seen to be laid at this time, but the warm, newly-laid Cuckoo egg was found with three cold eggs of the host.) There is perhaps some individual variation in laying time: Cuckoo A laid mostly during 1600–1800 hours BST, whereas Successor to A laid mainly after 1800 hours. Working in Kent, Owen (1933) found that Cuckoos parasitizing Dunnocks laid mainly in the afternoon, especially during 1630–1730 hours BST, and in Hungary, Molnar (1944) reported that Cuckoos laid in Great Reed Warbler nests mainly in the afternoon or early evening, but occasionally before noon. On the other hand, Baker (1942) stated that in India most cuckoos laid either early in the morning or in the afternoon and evening, but he gave no details. In the majority of known cases, egg-laying by parasitic cuckoos took place in the afternoon or evening, and this must be regarded as the general rule.

Table 22 *Time in day (BST) of egg-laying by individual European Cuckoos*

Individual Cuckoo	Host species	Dawn–1200	1201–1400	1401–1600	1601–1800	1801–dusk	Source
Cuckoo A	Meadow Pipit	2	3	14	28	1	Chance 1940
Successor to A	Meadow Pipit				3	18	Chance 1940
Cuckoo S	Meadow Pipit				4	2	Chance 1940
Cuckoo L	Meadow Pipit				1	1	Chance 1940
Cuckoo N	Meadow Pipit				1	1	Chance 1940
Cambridgeshire 77BN	Meadow Pipit				1		Present study
7	Meadow Pipit					1	Humphreys 1924
Cambridgeshire 74P	Reed Warbler			1			Present study
74B	Reed Warbler				3	5	Present study
74S	Reed Warbler				1		Present study
75C	Reed Warbler			2	1	2	Present study
75B	Reed Warbler					1	Present study
75BP	Reed Warbler					1	Present study
78BLBS	Reed Warbler				2	1	Present study
78GBL	Reed Warbler					1	Present study
79OB	Reed Warbler				1		Present study
79C	Reed Warbler			1	4	2	Present study
18	Yellowhammer					3	Chance 1940
19	Whinchat			1			Chance 1940
20	Dunnock					1	Chance 1940
21	Dunnock				1		Oundle School report
22	Pied Wagtail				1		Lancum 1925
23	Pied Wagtail					1	Barrington 1926
24	Redstart				1		Menzel 1970
25	Marsh Warbler				2	1	K. Gartner (pers. comm.)
TOTAL (120)		2	3	19	53	43	

The egg-laying interval (time between successive eggs) for individual European Cuckoos was shown by Chance to be about two days rather than one day like most small birds. Of 68 positively known egg-laying dates for two of Chance's Cuckoos parasitizing Meadow Pipits, 61 eggs were laid at intervals of two days, while only seven were laid at 3–5 days (Seel 1973). Other field workers in Europe and elsewhere have found a tendency for eggs to be laid at two-day intervals, but many eggs were probably overlooked because of the difficulty in finding them all. The female I followed by radio telemetry in 1979 probably laid her first egg in a Sedge Warbler nest on 28 May. She then laid at two-day intervals on 30 May, 1, 3, 5, 7, 9 and 11 June, always in Reed Warbler nests. On 13 June she spent a long time as usual at the reedbeds but was not seen to lay. She resumed two days later, laying a further three eggs on 15, 17 and 19 June. After this I could no longer keep close track of her, but I continued to find Reed Warbler nests in which another four of her eggs were laid on 29 June, 1, 5 and 10 July. This bird, to my knowledge, had produced three series consisting respectively of eight, three and four eggs during the course of a 45-day period (see below). An alternative way of determining egg-laying intervals was used by Payne (1973) working on nine species of African parasitic cuckoos. By examination of the ovaries of collected specimens, Payne confirmed the results of the field workers in that laying would occur every two days; only in some individuals of the smaller glossy cuckoos (*Chrysococcyx*), he thought, could laying occur at less than 48-hour intervals.

Laying in the afternoon or evening rather than in the morning, and laying at two-day intervals rather than on consecutive days, allow parasitic cuckoos to retain their eggs for unusually long periods. This is an advantage to the parasite in several ways: firstly, it allows the female plenty of time to find the nest if she does not know its exact location, or to find a replacement nest in the event of a nest loss. Secondly the cuckoo can wait until the hosts are away from their nest before flying to it to lay. Thirdly, it gives the female a longer period to form her egg, which could be important if she has to spend a lot of time finding nests and not feeding. Lastly, and most remarkably, it has been shown that freshly laid eggs of parasitic cuckoos are already slightly incubated, and this means that they will usually hatch before any of the host's eggs. For the Jacobin Cuckoo, *Clamator jacobinus*, Liversidge (1961) found that a freshly laid egg had a primitive embryonic streak equivalent to about 17–20 hours development compared to that of a chicken's egg, and Perrins (1967) found a visible embryo in a fresh European Cuckoo's egg taken from an unincubated nest of a Great Reed Warbler. Claudon (1955) also found incubated Cuckoo eggs in Reed Warbler nests where no incubation had occurred, but he wrongly interpreted this as evidence that the Cuckoo could move its eggs from nest to nest depending on whether or not the hosts accepted them.

One final aspect of the egg-laying procedure in cuckoos concerns the male. In European Cuckoos, the males apparently take no part in assisting females during egg-laying. There is no evidence to suggest that they indicate nests to females or that they take any notice of eggs or young. In a few other parasitic cuckoos the male does assist the female. His main task apparently is to distract the hosts which may be large, aggressive or group-nesting birds that could easily defend their nests against one female. There is some evidence that these cuckoos advertise their presence to the hosts for some time prior to parasitizing the nest – familiarization in this way may further reduce aggression towards the laying female and her egg.

Egg-laying seasonality

The timing and duration of the laying period in parasitic cuckoos is probably influenced by both food and host nest availability. The European Cuckoo arrives in its breeding range mostly in late April when some of its hosts have already started to breed. British Cuckoos, for example, do not start laying generally until about three weeks after they arrive, so they miss the early nests of Dunnocks, Meadow Pipits and Robins. Lack (1968) suggested that these three weeks were needed to build up energy reserves before producing eggs. If, in those first few weeks, Cuckoos experienced a shortage of their particular food, the subsequent laying season could be delayed, greatly reduced, or completely excluded. The hosts, on the other hand, because they do not have such a specialized diet, could breed more or less as normal.

Cuckoos stop laying in late June or early July and are the first summer visitors to leave Europe for Africa. Lack (1968) again proposed that they stopped laying so early because their food supply dwindled in late June. I find this hard to believe, however, because there appears to be a good supply of hairy caterpillars in most habitats until August or even later, and fledged young Cuckoos are known to feed mainly on large typical caterpillars in August and September. Clearly some quantitative data are required on this point.

The start and end of laying by some Cuckoos seems to coincide with the availability of host nests. Cuckoos parasitizing Reed Warblers in my study started laying in each year usually when the very first nests contained eggs and continued until as late as mid-July. Host nests were available until even later than this, often into August. Cuckoos parasitiz-

1 and 2   A female Cuckoo, *Cuculus canorus*, (code name 78GBL) arrives at a Reed Warbler's, *Acrocephalus scirpaceus*, nest at 1809 hours BST on 12 June 1978 at Woodwalton, Cambridgeshire. She picks out one of the three warbler's eggs and holds it in her bill

3   Still holding the Reed Warbler's egg, the female Cuckoo raises her abdomen over the nest to lay her egg. She then flies off immediately without seeing her egg, the whole operation taking as little as ten seconds

4 and 5   Another female Cuckoo (code name 74B) arrives at a Reed Warbler's nest at 1620 hours BST on 3 July 1975 at St Ives, Cambridgeshire. This female laid nine eggs usually at two-day intervals in 1975 and occupied the study area during five seasons, 1974–1978

6 The Cuckoo's feet remain on the edge of the nest while she lays her egg. The warbler's egg held during the laying will be taken away and eaten

7, 8, 9 and 10   Four eggs laid by different female Cuckoos in Reed Warbler nests during 1974-1979 in Cambridgeshire. Two show good resemblance to the colour of the host's eggs, while two show poor mimicry

11 Usually between 8 and 36 hours after hatching the young Cuckoo instinctively ejects any eggs or young in the nest. It has a small hollow in its back which traps an egg against the nest wall while the Cuckoo climbs backwards to the rim where the eggs will be rolled out one by one

12 After 18 days in the nest the young Cuckoo weighs about five times the weight of one of the Reed Warblers and is almost ready to fledge. The hosts constantly bring food, attracted by the incessant begging cries and bright orange-red gape of the youngster

13   One of the experimentally marked Cuckoos (code name 75B) was violently
attacked by up to eight neighbouring Sedge Warblers, *Acrocephalus schoenobaenus*
while approaching a Reed Warbler's nest to lay

14   Despite such attack, she reached the nest and exchanged the single Reed
Warbler's egg for one of her own. The Reed Warbler's only response was to burst
into song nearby. Another female Cuckoo was watching these proceedings from a
bush close by. Some time within the following two days the Cuckoo's egg
disappeared – probably robbed by the second female

15   An experimentally wing-tagged young Cuckoo (code name 77D) marked just before it could fly. This bird came back to its natal area in the following two years and proved to be a male. *Photo: R. K. Murton*

ing Meadow Pipits studied by Chance, however, started laying after the first pipit nests held eggs, but stopped when no more nests were available. On a broader scale, using the laying dates of 717 Cuckoo eggs found by A. E. Lees and Guy Charteris, Lack (1963) showed that Cuckoos parasitizing five different hosts in Britain laid most of their eggs during slightly different periods. First was the Robin, mainly 1 May–4 June, followed by the Dunnock, 8 May–11 June; Sedge Warbler, 15 May–2 July; Pied Wagtail, 22 May–25 June; and Reed Warbler, 29 May–2 July.

The laying season of Cuckoos, therefore, appears to be proximally timed to coincide with the peak laying period of the different host species. In general, Cuckoos which parasitize early-nesting species such as the resident Robin or Dunnock lay earlier than those parasitizing later-nesting ones such as migrant warblers.

For the record, the earliest known Cuckoo egg that I have been able to find was reported by J. Harper in the nest of a Dunnock on 5 April 1851 (Jourdain 1924). We now have no way of assessing its validity. Many other records of Cuckoo eggs in April are available, mostly in Robin or Dunnock nests, and mostly towards the end of the month. Cuckoos laying at more southerly latitudes within Europe possibly lay earlier than in the north, but I have seen no detailed records. The latest recorded egg was found on 22 July in a Reed Warbler's nest in the Netherlands (Paulussen 1957), but its state of incubation was not recorded: it could have been laid on 10 July. Similarly, A. E. Lees (in Lack 1963) recorded an egg in a Dunnock nest on 20 July. Scholey (1927) recorded an egg laid in a Reed Warbler nest on 12 July. The latest Cuckoo egg that I have found in this host species in Cambridgeshire was laid on 14 July by a bird (78BLBS) which started laying on 2 June (Table 23). In fact, the bird was photographed on this occasion from a hide placed about 2.5m from a nest containing three eggs. She arrived at the nest, ate two of the host's eggs, picked up the other in her bill and laid. But her egg missed the nest and landed undamaged on the ground 1m below and 1m to one side. She flew off with the third egg leaving the nest empty. In Meadow Pipit nests the latest egg-laying recorded by Chance (1940) was 30 June, while in France, the latest egg found by Blaise (1965) in Robin nests was laid on 17 June. A dubious record of a fresh egg in a Greenfinch nest on 2 August 1882 was reported by de la Comble (1958).

The overall egg-laying period in European Cuckoos, therefore, appears to be about 12 weeks, similar to that found in tropical parasitic cuckoos and North American non-parasitic cuckoos. An individual, however, is unlikely to lay over a period exceeding six or seven weeks.

Table 23 *Laying seasons of individual female Cuckoos, Cuculus canorus*
Dates in parentheses were estimated

Individual	Year	Host	Extreme dates between eggs	No. eggs	No. days	Source
Cuckoo A	1918	Meadow Pipit	28.5–23.6	9 (+2 young)	27	Chance 1940
	1919	Meadow Pipit	18.5–23.6	16 (+2 young)	37	Chance 1940
	1920	Meadow Pipit	13.5–27.6	21	46	Chance 1940
	1921	Meadow Pipit	12.5–13.6	15	33	Chance 1940
	1922	Meadow Pipit	11.5–29.6	25	50	Chance 1940
Cuckoo B	1918	Meadow Pipit	14.6–22.6	4	9	Chance 1940
	1919	Meadow Pipit	28.6–30.6	2	3	Chance 1940
Cuckoo N	1921	Meadow Pipit	(14.6)–(20.6)	2	7	Chance 1940
	1922	Meadow Pipit	(1.6)–(22.6)	3	22	Chance 1940
	1923	Meadow Pipit	(31.5)–(16.6)	9	17	Chance 1940
	1924	Meadow Pipit	13.5–5.6	9	24	Chance 1940
Cuckoo S	1921	Meadow Pipit	19.5–18.6	14	31	Chance 1940
Successor to A	1924	Meadow Pipit	3.6–15.6	7	13	
	1925	Meadow Pipit	10.5–15.6	14	37	
no. 6	1921	Reed Warbler	14.5–6.7	19	54	G. Scholey in Chance 1940
no. 7	1927	Reed Warbler	(21.5)–12.7	16	53	Scholey 1927
no. 8	1921	Reed Warbler	1.6–28.6	11	28	E. E. Pettit in Chance 1940
no. 9	1921	Reed Warbler	29.5–15.6	7	18	A. E. Lees in Chance 1940

74P	1974	Reed Warbler	(22.5)–3.6	6	13	Present study (Cambs. 1974–1979)
74BL	1974	Reed Warbler	(6.6)–(6.7)	4	31	Present study
74G	1974	Reed Warbler	12.6–16.6	2	5	Present study
74B	1974	Reed Warbler	(1.6)–11.7	12	41	Present study
	1975	Reed Warbler	(9.6)–3.7	9	25	Present study
	1976	Reed Warbler	(19.5)–4.6	3	17	Present study
	1978	Reed Warbler	(26.5)–20.6	6	26	Present study
75P	1975	Reed Warbler	(24.5)–(5.7)	12	43	Present study
75C	1975	Reed Warbler	6.6–(8.7)	9	33	Present study
76GB	1977	Reed Warbler	(15.6)–(29.6)	3	15	Present study
78BLBS	1978	Reed Warbler	(2.6)–14.7	15	43	Present study
	1979	Reed Warbler	(31.5)–(10.7)	15	41	Present study
78BLFB	1978	Reed Warbler	(27.6)–(8.7)	3	12	Present study
	1979	Reed Warbler	10.6–(29.6)	6	20	Present study
78RHCP	1978	Reed Warbler	(17.6)–(5.7)	8	19	Present study
78GBL	1978	Reed Warbler	(23.5)–20.6	11	29	Present study
79C	1979	Reed Warbler	(28.5)–(10.7)	15	44	Present study
79OB	1979	Reed Warbler	3.6–25.6	7	23	Present study
79PBL	1979	Reed Warbler	6.6–(26.6)	4	21	Present study
no. 30	1921	Sedge Warbler	14.5–27.6	10	45	A. E. Lees in Chance 1940
no. 31	1924	Yellowhammer	(21.5)–26.6	14	37	Chance 1940
no. 32	1923	Spotted Flycatcher	(1.6)–(23.6)	7	23	Chance 1940
			MEAN =	9.2	27.7	

The egg-laying periods of many individual female Cuckoos that were identified from their unique eggs and which laid more than one egg in a season are shown in Table 23. The data are taken only from workers who concentrated on Cuckoos parasitizing particular hosts in given areas, but do not take into account any eggs that they may have missed. The great variability in egg-laying periods reflects the inability of observers to find all the eggs, but also suggests that different Cuckoos have different egg-laying potential, and that the same female may lay over longer or shorter periods in different years. Thus I found 12 eggs laid by Cuckoo 74B in 41 days in 1974, but 9 eggs in 25 days, 3 in 17, 1 only, and 6 in 26 days in the following four years. There were plenty of nests available each year. The data from individual females in Table 23 give a mean egg-laying period of 27.7 days, undoubtedly an underestimate because of the difficulty in finding all the eggs laid by each bird.

Chance destroyed Meadow Pipit nests which had been parasitized or had gone beyond a stage suitable for parasitism, thus experimentally providing a succession of nests by inducing the hosts to build again. In the 1921 season, he deliberately stopped the supply of nests after 13 June and found no more of his Cuckoo A's eggs on the common that year. He interpreted this as evidence that the availability of nests limited the number of eggs and length of a Cuckoo's breeding season. He did not consider the possibility that his bird went elsewhere to lay or used some other host species, although in the next year she returned to the same place and laid again in pipit nests.

In contrast, I have found that the number of Reed Warbler nests available for Cuckoos to parasitize each year was always higher than the number actually used by Cuckoos in Cambridgeshire, even at small breeding sites. The proportions of nests parasitized in different years and at seven different sites in Cambridgeshire are shown in Table 24. Overall, the frequency of nests parasitized ranged from 0 to 38.1 per cent, while at my main study area (site 1), a proportion of 3.3 – 23.4 per cent of nests were victimized in the six years. The higher proportions were found mainly at smaller sites where there were fewer host nests, or in years when many females were present. Examining the results for site 1, Table 24 shows that in 1976 and 1977 the proportion of nests parasitized was much lower than in the other years. Severe drought conditions prevailed in 1976 (mean June temperature = 17.0°C), whereas 1977 was cold and wet (mean June temperature = 11.9°C). The inference was that abnormal temperatures in June, the Cuckoo's main laying period, reduced the food supply, with a result that fewer eggs were laid. On the other hand, while the parasitism was low at site 1 in 1977, it was high at site 2 some 18km away, suggesting that food was plentiful there.

Table 24 *Parasitism frequencies of Reed Warbler nests at seven sites in Cambridgeshire 1974–1979*

Site	Year	No. of female* Cuckoos	Number nests with eggs	Number nests parasitized	%	Mean June temperature**
1	1974	6	107	25	23.4	13.8
	1975	8	208	34	16.4	13.8
	1976	3	119	5	4.2	17.0
	1977	3	182	6	3.3	11.9
	1978	3	219	24	11.0	13.6
	1979	3	247	22	8.9	13.8
2	1977	2	29	7	24.1	11.9
	1978	2	52	11	21.2	13.6
3	1978	1	21	8	38.1	13.6
	1979	1	18	3	16.7	13.8
4	1978	1	17	1	5.9	13.6
	1979	4	59	12	20.3	13.8
5	1979	2	55	10	18.2	13.8
6	1979	1	19	2	10.5	13.8
7	1979	0	5	0	0	13.8
	TOTAL/MEAN		1,367	170	12.4	

* Identified by egg-colour
** From records at Monks Wood Nature Reserve, Cambridgeshire

Further research, taking into account weather conditions, food supply and host-nest availability, is desperately needed to investigate this important problem.

Number of eggs laid

The record for number of eggs laid in one season by a parasitic cuckoo is held by Chance's Cuckoo A which, under experimental conditions, laid 25 eggs in 1922. Table 23 gives the number of eggs laid by individual Cuckoos which laid more than one egg in a season, giving a mean of 9.2 eggs for the 46 Cuckoo-years. Excluded from these data are the many birds which were found by these different observers to lay only one egg in a season. Some of these may have been host-specific birds remaining in the same area during the breeding season, while others may have laid casually in no fixed area. Although suffering a considerable observer bias, the results suggest that a prolific female Cuckoo lays 10–20 (up to 25) eggs in a season lasting 3–7 weeks. Other individuals lay up to 9 or 10 eggs in a 1–5 week season, while many others lay only 1 or 2 eggs.

Field studies of breeding Cuckoos have shown that eggs tend to be laid in series or 'clutches', with longer breaks than two days between successive eggs. Table 25 gives data for Chance's Cuckoo A in 1918–1922 and for the female, mentioned earlier, that I followed by radio telemetry in 1979. The number of eggs laid in series was very variable. Using histological techniques, Payne (1973, 1974) also found 'clutches' in African parasitic cuckoos with a mean clutch size of 3.48 eggs in eight species. He found this to be significantly higher than the mean clutch size (2.82) in 39 species of non-parasitic cuckoos. Presumably, breaks in the laying sequence of more than two days allow female cuckoos even more time to find host nests or form their eggs. Most of the gaps in egg-laying sequences were of four days suggesting that one egg was either missed by the observer or aborted by the Cuckoo.

The laying histories of several individual Cuckoos (identified by their egg-types) are tabulated in Table 26, giving the number of eggs laid during successive years. There is no apparent difference in reproductive effort at different ages. Cuckoo A, for example, laid the largest number of eggs in its last year, whereas Cuckoo 74B laid more in her first year of encounter. In African species, Payne (1973) also found no significant difference in the number of eggs laid by first-year and older females. It is not always possible to age cuckoos after the first moult, since only some first-year birds retain a few juvenile feathers. Three of my wing-tagged young male Cuckoos returned in the following year of their birth to their respective natal sites in Cambridgeshire. They sang

Table 25   *Number of eggs laid in series or clutches by individual Cuckoos*

Individual	Year	Number of eggs in series with number of days between 'clutches' in parentheses						No. of eggs
Cuckoo A	1918	4	(4)	6	(6)	1		11
(Chance 1940)	1919	5	(4)	13				18
	1920	16	(4)	4	(5)	1		21
	1921	5	(4)	5	(4)	5		15
	1922	2	(3)	23				25
Cuckoo 79C (present study)	1979	8	(4)	3	(10)	4		15

Table 26 *Numbers of eggs laid by individual Cuckoos in successive years*

Individual	Host species	Years (no.)	No. eggs/year	Source
Cuckoo A	Meadow Pipit	1918–1922 (5)	11;18;21;15;25	Chance 1940
Cuckoo N	Meadow Pipit	1921–1924 (4)	2;3;9;9	Chance 1940
74B	Reed Warbler	1974–1978 (5)	12;9;3;1;6	Present study
78BLBS	Reed Warbler	1978–1979 (2)	15;15	
78BLFB	Reed Warbler	1978–1979 (2)	3;6	
no. 6	Reed Warbler	(3)	15;16;15	P. Bunyard in Baker 1942
no. 7	Reed Warbler	1925–1927 (3)	16;15;16	Scholey 1927
no. 8	Red-backed Shrike	1889–1892 (4)	5;8;9;7	Rey 1892
no. 9	Fantail Warbler	1925–1935 (11)	6;8;14;9;10;12; 15;18;14;11;15	Baker 1942

and courted females, indicating that some birds, at least, try to breed as yearlings. No wing-tagged yearling females were found to lay eggs but Seel (in prep.) has one record of a museum yearling female containing an oviduct egg.

There are a number of records of individual female Cuckoos laying eggs over consecutive years, giving some indication of their egg-laying lives (Table 27). The most complete record was supplied by Blaise (1965) in a 12-year study in north-east France of Cuckoos parasitizing Reed Warblers. By their distinct egg-types, he identified no less than 44 female Cuckoos during the study. Thirty of them laid in only one season, many of them laying just a single egg. The average egg-laying life of a Cuckoo calculated from Table 27 is 2.1 years but this includes all the one-season birds which may have been itinerant or not host-specific and therefore overlooked. Also, some Cuckoos were not followed up in future years by the recorders. Generally, it would seem that a dominant female Cuckoo in Europe might lay over four or five years, but occasionally up to eight years. In India, Baker (1942) recorded one female Cuckoo of the race *bakeri* parasitizing warblers in a small area over 11 consecutive years (Table 26).

Laying more than one egg in a nest

Parasitic cuckoos which lay eggs in the nests of small host species all lay only one egg into each nest. There are a few records of individual cuckoos laying in the same nest twice, but these were apparently in desperation when no other nests were available. All students of European Cuckoo eggs have remarked that multiple eggs in one nest were invariably the product of different females. Two to four, or even five, Cuckoo eggs have been found in Great Reed Warbler nests in Hungary

Table 27 *Records of egg-laying years of individual Cuckoos, Cuculus canorus*

Years	No. of years	No. of Cuckoos or code name	Host species	Notes	Source
1918–1922	5	1 (Cuckoo A)	Meadow Pipit	Worcestershire; thought 1918 was first year	Chance 1940
1921–1924	4	1 (Cuckoo N)	Meadow Pipit	Worcestershire	Chance 1940
1959–1964	5	1	Dunnock	Denmark	C. F. Christiansen in Blair 1965
?	5	1	Dunnock	Kent	Owen 1933
1951–1957	7	1	Reed Warbler	France	Labitte 1957
(1952–1963)	8	1	Reed Warbler	France; 12 year study; 44 Cuckoos	Blaise 1965
	7	2			
	6	1			
	5	2			
	4	1			
	3	2			
	2	5			
	1	30			
(1974–1979)	5	1 (74B)	Reed Warbler	Cambridgeshire; present study; 25 Cuckoos	
	2	7			
	1	17			
1956–1958	3	1	Robin	France	Blaise 1965
1889–1892	4	1	Red-backed Shrike	Leipzig, Germany	Rey 1892

Cuckoo species	Host	Region	No. of nests parasitized	With 2+ cuckoo eggs	%	Source
(a) *non-ejector species*						
Jacobin Cuckoo, *Clamator jacobinus*	(Mainly bulbuls)	Africa	114	8	7	Friedmann 1964
	Cape Bulbul	Africa	41	9	22	Liversidge 1971
	Babblers	Asia	106	22	21	Baker 1942
	Babblers	India	55	19	34	Gaston 1976
Red-winged Crested Cuckoo, *Clamator coromandus*	Laughingthrushes	Asia	171	32	19	Baker 1942
	Laughingthrushes	India	6	6	100	Osmaston 1916
Great Spotted Cuckoo, *Clamator glandarius*	Crows	S Europe–N Africa	43	10	23	Friedmann 1964
	Crows	S Africa	35	30	86	Friedmann 1964
	Crows	Total range	172	90	52	Friedmann 1964
	Magpie	Spain	28	18	64	J. D. Macdonald in Friedmann 1964
Striped Crested Cuckoo, *Clamator levaillanti*	Pied Crow	Nigeria	9	8	89	Mundy & Cook 1977
	Babblers	Africa	23	3	13	Friedmann 1964
Koel, *Eudynamis scolopacea*	Crows	Asia	91	55	60	Baker 1942
(b) *ejector species*						
Cuckoo, *Cuculus canorus*	Meadow Pipit	Worcestershire, GB	86	5	5.8	Chance 1940
	Red-backed Shrike	Leipzig, Germany	?42	28	67	Rey 1894
	Great Reed Warbler	Hungary	312	139	44	Molnar 1944
	Great Reed Warbler	France	30	3	10	De Chavigny 1934
	Reed Warbler	France	223	2	0.9	Blaise 1965
	Reed Warbler	Cambridgeshire, GB	170	6	3.5	Present study (1974–1979)
C. canorus bakeri	All hosts	Germany	1,246	51	4.1	Rey 1892
	All hosts	India	2,068	46	2.2	Baker 1942

(Molnar 1944). Two females laid in the same nest (though not on the same days) on only six occasions during six years in Cambridgeshire; in three instances the second-laying female removed the egg laid by the first. The habit could, therefore, be easily overlooked.

In larger parasitic cuckoos, where the laying details are known, more than one egg may be laid by an individual into the same nest on a more regular basis. The hosts of these species can usually rear a young cuckoo alongside their own young, and the parasite does not eject its nest-mates, which might include one of its own kin. The crested *Clamator* cuckoos and the Koel are well-known to lay more than one egg in each host nest: up to 16 Koel eggs have been found in a nest of the House Crow, *Corvus splendens*, in India, and up to 10 eggs of the Great Spotted Cuckoo, *Clamator glandarius*, have been found in one Pied Crow's, *Corvus albus*, nest. However, it has not been shown whether these eggs were all laid by the same females. Table 28 gives some records for the crested cuckoos and Koel, compared with the details collected for the Cuckoo. The high values for European Cuckoos parasitizing Great Reed Warblers and Red-backed Shrikes probably arose because of very high local densities of Cuckoos.

9 | Eggs

Such a great deal of attention has been paid to the eggs of parasitic cuckoos in the past that ornithological literature abounds with details and interpretations of them. Due to egg-collectors until very recent times, thousands of eggs were collected, along with those of the species in whose nests they were found. As a private collector, Baker (1942) boasted a collection of nearly 6,000 cuckoo eggs, many from Europe, but mostly from Asiatic cuckoo species in India and surrounding countries. It soon became apparent to early collectors that cuckoo eggs resembled their host's eggs too often for this similarity to be merely coincidental. With the widespread acceptance of Darwin's theory of evolution by natural selection, it became clear that such a process had resulted in cuckoo eggs matching those of their hosts; this was explained in great detail by Baker in his book, *Cuckoo Problems*. He was perhaps better qualified than anyone else before him to discuss the evolution of cuckoo eggs. Even today, his work remains an authoritative document on the subject, despite the fact that some of his identifications of eggs are now known to be wrong (Lack 1968). Some of Baker's ideas have been modified in the light of more recent research, but the essential hypothesis, that mimetic eggs evolved through discrimination by the hosts, remains undisputed.

As a general rule, parasitic cuckoo eggs are comparatively small, both in size and weight, in relation to the size of bird. They are also thick-shelled, and highly variable or polymorphic in colour. Each of these features has been regarded as an adaptation towards brood parasitism: reduction in size to allow parasitism of a wide range of smaller and more abundant host species, and colour mimicry to avoid rejection of eggs by the hosts.

Egg size

The evidence for a reduction in size of parasitic cuckoo eggs can be seen by comparing their size in relation to body size with those of nesting cuckoos (Figure 9). In nearly every case, eggs of the parasites are proportionally smaller. The main exceptions – the Great Spotted Cuckoo, Koel, and Channel-billed Cuckoo – all parasitize hosts of similar relative size: these cuckoos, therefore, do not require small eggs, either for proper incubation or to avoid rejection by the hosts.

Eggs of European Cuckoos average slightly larger than those of the hosts (Table 29). On average they are about 2mm longer and broader than the average host egg. They are also rounder in appearance. Latter (1902, 1905) and Baker (1942) compared egg sizes according to different host species of European Cuckoos in an attempt to show that each gens laid eggs of corresponding size to the eggs of its particular host. Naturally, they expected to find that Cuckoo eggs would be larger with larger hosts and smaller with smaller ones. Instead, they found no correlation, except Cuckoo eggs found in nests of leaf-warblers and wrens – the smallest hosts – were slightly smaller than the average, though still larger than the host's eggs (Table 29). At the other extreme, Cuckoo eggs from the nests of Red-backed Shrikes averaged slightly less than the mean shrike-egg size, although they were the same as the Cuckoo's overall mean egg size. No recent analysis of Cuckoo egg-size has been made, one of the problems being that many eggs now in museums are of doubtful host origin.

In the case of the European Cuckoo, therefore, no strong correlation between egg size and host specificity has yet been found. In the Asiatic Large Hawk-Cuckoo, *Cuculus sparverioides*, however, Baker found two egg-types associated with two different groups of hosts, and here there was a size difference. Large Hawk-Cuckoo eggs from nests of spider-hunters (*Arachnothera*) and shortwings (*Brachypteryx*) were brown, like those of the hosts, and averaged 26.3 × 18.5mm in size. Those found in the nests of laughingthrushes (*Garrulax*), laying larger blue eggs, were also blue but averaged 29.0 × 20.5mm. This suggests that host specialization has resulted in different sized eggs in the same cuckoo species.

Egg weight

Among nidicolous land birds (birds with undeveloped young at hatching), the cuckoo family shows extremes in the relationship of egg weight to body weight (Lack 1968). The Crotophaginae subfamily lay proportionally heavy eggs, an ani's egg weighing about 20–25 per cent of the adult weight, while most parasitic cuckoos (Cuculinae) lay proportionally low weight eggs at only about 5 per cent of the adult weight. A European Cuckoo's egg, for example, weighs about 3.4g (range 2.9–

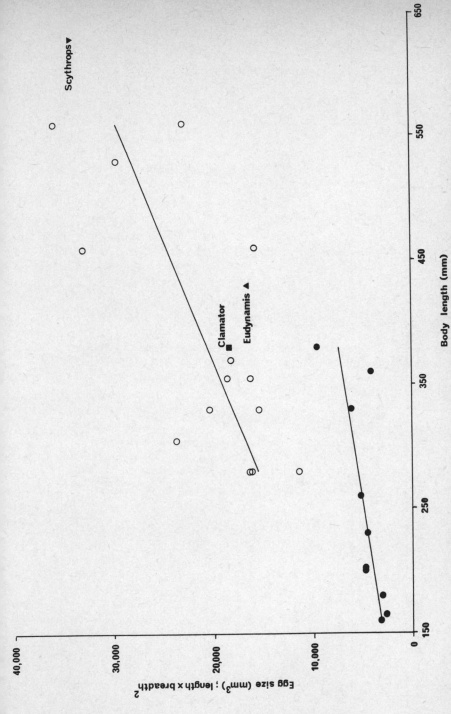

Figure 9. Comparison of egg size and body size between parasitic (closed symbols) and non-parasitic (open circles) cuckoos

Table 29 *Mean dimensions (length × breadth) of eggs of European Cuckoos and different host species*

Host species	Host egg size (mm) (from Harrison 1975)	Cuckoo egg size (mm)				Mean shell weight (mg) (Baker 1942)
		(Latter 1905)	n	(Baker 1942)	n	
Meadow Pipit, *Anthus pratensis*	19.8 × 14.6	22.3 × 16.6	86	22.7 × 16.6[1]	151	219
Tree Pipit, *Anthus trivialis*	20.7 × 15.6	22.6 × 16.6	48			
Pied Wagtail, *Motacilla alba* }	20.6 × 15.3	22.3 × 16.5	85	22.7 × 16.7	116	214
White Wagtail, *Motacilla alba* }		22.4 × 16.7	115			
Red-backed Shrike, *Lanius collurio*	22.9 × 17.1	22.3 × 16.5	307	22.3 × 16.4[2]	45	240
Dunnock, *Prunella modularis*	19.9 × 14.7	22.6 × 16.8	58	22.4 × 16.3	122	220
Reed Warbler, *Acrocephalus scirpaceus*	18.4 × 13.6	22.6 × 16.6	66	22.7 × 17.3	188	244
Marsh Warbler, *Acrocephalus palustris*	19.9 × 14.2	22.1 × 16.3	37			
Great Reed Warbler, *A. arundinaceus*	22.6 × 16.2			22.6 × 15.9	247	245
Sedge Warbler, *A. schoenobaenus*	17.7 × 13.1	22.1 × 16.4	48			
Whitethroat, *Sylvia communis*	18.6 × 13.9	21.8 × 16.2	37			
Garden Warbler, *Sylvia borin*	20.1 × 14.8	21.9 × 16.4	91	22.5 × 16.5[3]	264	219
Barred Warbler, *Sylvia nisoria*	21.1 × 14.4	21.8 × 16.3	35			
Redstart, *Phoenicurus phoenicurus*	18.6 × 13.7	22.4 × 16.6	64	21.9 × 16.4[4]	40	220
Robin, *Erithacus rubecula*	19.9 × 15.4	22.8 × 16.8	78	22.2 × 15.6	100	214
Wren, *Troglodytes troglodytes*	17.6 × 13.3	21.4 × 16.2	54	22.0 × 16.1	63	218
Yellowhammer, *Emberiza citrinella*	21.6 × 15.3	22.2 × 16.5	31	22.9 × 16.8[5]	67	218
MEAN 15 species =	19.8 × 14.6	22.3 × 16.5	1,572	22.2 × 16.5	1,592	219.5

Notes
[1] All pipits
[2] All shrikes
[3] Miscellaneous warblers
[4] Mostly Redstart-Cuckoo eggs, but not all

3.8g for 31 freshly laid eggs in Reed Warbler nests), representing a mere 3 per cent of the adult female weight. The egg weight to body weight ratio in most of the Cuckoo's host species is about 10 per cent. Payne (1974) plotted the relationship between egg weight and body weight in the cuckoo family as a whole, showing that parasitic cuckoo eggs were mostly of lower relative weight than those of nesting species of similar size. As with egg size in the last section, the main exception here was the Great Spotted Cuckoo which does not require a smaller egg.

I have found that egg weights of individual birds vary little during a season. Chance (1922), however, noted that the shell weights of the eggs laid by his Cuckoo A increased during the season, and decreased towards the last egg of each year. The possibility that egg weights as well as egg sizes vary according to host species needs further critical study.

It has been well established that there is a direct correlation between egg weight and chick weight at hatching in most birds, and that egg weights relative to body weights are broadly characteristic for each species (Lack 1968). In general, birds which lay large eggs relative to body weight produce more advanced chicks at hatching than birds which lay small eggs. The young resulting from the larger eggs of nesting species of American cuckoos hatch in a more advanced state than young parasitic cuckoos. They have a loose covering of down, their eyes open quickly, they develop rapidly, and soon leave the nest for the relative safety of the surrounding bushes or vegetation. The young of parasitic cuckoo species, on the contrary, hatch naked and blind, and remain in the nest for a longer period.

Egg colour and mimicry

The colours and markings of cuckoo eggs are probably more variable than in any other bird family. This variability has been attributed to the evolution of cuckoo eggs to mimic those of their respective hosts. Non-parasitic cuckoos, like the American Yellow- and Black-billed Cuckoos, lay white, pale blue or greenish eggs, often covered with a white chalky deposit. Such colours are thought to be the most primitive in modern birds because they represent little advance from the white eggs of bird's ancestors – the reptiles.

Examples of egg-mimicry in parasitic cuckoos can be found in all the genera so far studied, but not in all species. Perhaps the most simple, though equally effective, forms of mimicry are shown by those cuckoos which lay unmarked white or pale blue eggs with hosts laying similar eggs. Examples include the Jacobin and Red-winged Crested Cuckoos in Asia, laying clear blue eggs with babblers and laughingthrushes. At the other extreme, some striking resemblances occur in species which parasitize hosts that lay intricately marked and coloured eggs. The Asiatic Koel, for example, parasitizing mainly the House Crow, *Corvus splendens*, lays strongly mimetic eggs, even faithfully copying different colour shades of crow eggs across India (Baker 1942). Similarly, the Great Spotted Cuckoo is restricted to parasitizing Magpies in southern Europe, where it lays eggs coloured and marked almost exactly like those of the host. When a cuckoo species is restricted to using one main host species or group of hosts laying similar eggs, as in the above examples, egg-mimicry has become highly developed. In fact, eggs of such cuckoos often can be identified only by an expert who has to consider shape, shell thickness, texture, and weight before a cuckoo egg can be safely recorded. Egg-collectors have occasionally noted that clutches sent to them have contained cuckoo eggs so well-matched that their finders had completely overlooked them.

Most parasitic cuckoos use only a few main host species (Chapter 7), but their eggs are found in the nests of a large number of others. With the main hosts egg-mimicry is usually good, sometimes excellent, while in the others it is less apparent or absent. The European Cuckoo, which has attracted the most attention, tends to lay mimetic eggs in the nests of several of its main hosts. The best examples are found with Redstarts, Bramblings, Great Reed Warblers, and possibly Garden Warblers. In central and eastern Europe, these seem to be the predominant egg-types. Occasionally they are found with other hosts, and the degree of mimicry becomes more a matter of chance. For example, clear blue Cuckoo eggs which are normally found in Redstart nests are sometimes laid in nests of Pied Flycatchers or Wheatears which also have blue eggs; mimicry is therefore maintained. Similarly, Cuckoos parasitizing Red-backed Shrikes in Germany lay eggs similar to their host's eggs, but these are not unlike the more common type found in nests of Garden Warblers throughout central Europe. Great Reed Warbler-Cuckoos in Hungary and elsewhere sometimes lay eggs in nests of Marsh Warblers with which their eggs do not contrast greatly. The European Cuckoo therefore has developed its egg-mimicry in certain places with particular hosts, but has also enjoyed success with other host species because their eggs have not differed in size and colour from the main hosts. In western Europe the main hosts are Meadow Pipits, Reed Warblers, Pied Wagtails and Dunnocks. The three former species themselves lay somewhat variable eggs and those Cuckoos which victimize them lay eggs which only approximately match the general egg-type. Mimicry can advance no further in these hosts. Cuckoo eggs laid in Dunnock nests, on the contrary, are totally unlike the brilliant blue eggs of the host, yet this species does not seem to discriminate against them. Baker proposed that insufficient time had elapsed for the evolution of a blue egg with this host, despite the fact that unmarked blue eggs had already evolved in Redstart nests elsewhere in Europe. Admittedly, Dunnocks may be comparatively recent hosts in north-west Europe as a result of their increase in numbers following the break-up of the habitat by cultivation; but their ready acceptance of ill-matched Cuckoo eggs makes it questionable whether blue Cuckoo eggs would ever evolve with this host.

In cuckoos with a wide range of hosts, the temptation is for us to look for accurate egg-mimicry in each host species. Rather, it would seem that cuckoos have only a few egg-types each equally suited to several hosts which lay eggs of the same type. Whichever host is the more abundant receives most of the cuckoo's attention. The situation is illustrated in two Asiatic cuckoos described by Baker (1923, 1942). The Lesser Cuckoo, *Cuculus poliocephalus*, ranging from the western Himalayas to Japan, lays eggs of two main types: white in the west of its range in nests of various warblers also laying white eggs, and chocolate-brown in the east with other warblers laying brown eggs. Where the two types meet in the middle of the cuckoo's range, there is considerable overlap and mis-matched eggs occur in the 'wrong' host nests. The Asiatic Large Hawk-Cuckoo, as already mentioned, also lays eggs of two main colour types with two kinds of hosts, but where they overlap in range, this cuckoo rarely lays eggs with the wrong host. In the first species, therefore, the two egg-types are kept geographically distinct, whereas in the latter, they are host-specifically separate.

Baker believed that the reason for different standards of cuckoo egg-mimicry with different host species was a result of the length of time that each species had been victimized: the longer the time, the better the mimicry. However, several examples can be found where this is not true. As described in Chapter 7, for instance, the genus of crested *Clamator* cuckoos is comprised of the oldest species, *C. jacobinus*, which in Africa lays unmarked white eggs which contrast with the spotted eggs of its bulbul hosts. The youngest species, according to Friedmann (1964), is *C. glandarius* which lays highly evolved eggs matching those of its Magpie hosts in Europe. In other words, the oldest member of the genus lays non-mimetic white eggs, while the most recent species in evolution lays beautifully marked mimetic ones.

It seems more likely that the degree of host discrimination against strange eggs in their nests produces the varying degrees of egg-mimicry in cuckoos. Host species which have accurate powers of egg-recognition and habitually reject mis-matched cuckoo eggs by deserting their nests or throwing out the odd egg, are only successfully parasitized by highly mimetic cuckoo eggs. At the other extreme, those host species which do not reject strange eggs, like the Dunnock, will accept non-mimetic eggs. Within a host population there will probably be some individuals which do discriminate and others which do not. The non-discriminators will be more successfully parasitized. More young of these, presumably not carrying the discriminating genes, are destroyed by the activities of the young cuckoo. Gradually, therefore, the discriminating members of a host population become more abundant, resulting in the more rapid evolution of mimetic cuckoo eggs.

Also affecting the degree of egg-mimicry in cuckoo eggs may be the amount of isolation enjoyed by each cuckoo species or each gens within a species. Southern (1954) proposed that in large areas of homogeneous habitat, such as the forests of eastern Europe and Scandinavia or the reedbeds of Hungary, each gens of the European Cuckoo could remain isolated, concentrating on one main host species and achieving good egg-mimicry. Where the European landscape has been broken up by cultivation, the gens have not remained separate, possibly resulting in a breakdown of egg-mimicry.

From the foregoing we can conclude that the degree of egg-mimicry has evolved (i) through the degree of discrimination by different hosts, and (ii) through the amount of isolation of each host-specific group of cuckoo and the length of time a host species has been exposed to parasitism.

Despite the fact that some species of cuckoo lay polymorphic eggs in order to parasitize different hosts, the eggs of an individual female are always identical. Baldamus (1868) was among the first to record this, and it has been subsequently verified, as we have seen earlier. This discovery was crucial to the field study of Cuckoos, since it has enabled workers such as Edgar Chance to identify one particular female during one and several seasons. If the eggs of an individual female were all differently coloured and marked, some of the important discoveries so far made on the breeding behaviour of the parasitic cuckoos would not have been possible.

It leads to the question of inheritance of egg-colour – an important aspect in the evolution of mimetic cuckoo eggs. For evolution to have occurred at all, young cuckoos must inherit their parent's egg colour. It was once thought that the male could carry a gene for egg-colour, and that cuckoos had to be careful in selecting mates with the same colour genes so that the eggs produced would be accepted by the hosts. Now it is thought that egg-colour is a sex-limited inherited gene carried only by the female. In this case the male has no influence on the egg-colour of his daughters, so that a promiscuous mating system and non-territorial social organization does not interfere with the genetic process of egg-mimicry. One of my objectives in wing-tagging a population of Cuckoos was to investigate this problem of egg-colour inheritance by examining the eggs of Cuckoos of known parent egg-type. Unfortunately, no eggs of marked young females were found, and only one wing-tagged female offspring was seen in a subsequent year in my study area. The possibilities for further research in this field are, therefore, still intriguing.

Incubation periods

As mentioned earlier, the eggs of some parasitic cuckoos are known to have partially developed embryos when they are laid because they have been incubated in the cuckoo's oviduct for a day. The meagre evidence for this would benefit from further corroborative data on a range of parasitic cuckoo eggs. It would also be interesting to know if a similar development occurs in the eggs of non-parasitic cuckoos.

For the European Cuckoo, most authorities give the 'incubation period' as 12–13 days. It would be more correct, however, to regard this time as the *laying to hatching period*. Since a Cuckoo's egg may be laid at any time during the host's clutch formation period, or even before the host starts laying, there may be a delay of 1–3 days before the foster-parent starts full-time incubation. Reed Warblers, for example, generally start full day and night incubation after the laying of their third egg, but there is probably individual variation in this with some birds starting to incubate after two eggs, others after four or five. So a Cuckoo's egg laid in the afternoon into a one-egg nest, will not be fully incubated until about 36–60 hours later. This does not mean that the embryo, which has already started to develop, dies from chilling. Lack (1956) found that a Swift's, *Apus apus*, egg could withstand cooling for two days without embryo death. Possibly the thick shell of a Cuckoo's egg plays a part in reducing heat loss both before and during incubation, perhaps contributing to the embryo's more rapid development.

The laying to hatching periods of nine Cuckoo eggs of known laying and hatching times in Reed Warbler nests are given in Table 30. One egg was laid on 2 July but removed from the nest and kept at room temperature for three days. It was returned to the nest on 5 July by which time incubation by the Reed Warblers had begun. The Cuckoo's egg hatched before any of the host's at 0600 hours BST on 17 July, giving an incubation period of only $11\frac{1}{2}$ days. For the nine eggs the mean laying to hatching time was 12.4 days, whereas incubation by the host (assuming

Table 30 *Laying to hatching periods of Cuckoo eggs laid in Reed Warbler nests*

Nest no.	Female Cuckoo	Date laid	Time (BST)	Date host started incubation[1]	Date hatched	Time (BST)	Laying–hatching (days)	Incubation–hatching (days)
R100	74B	17.6	1850	19.6	30.6	1310	12.8	11.3
R196	74B	3.7	1620	5.7	16.7	1700	12.9	11.5
R124	75C	15.6	1700	17.6	28.6	1855	13.1	11.5
R206	75P	5.7	1200[2]	4.7	17.7	0915	11.9	11.9
SW5	79C	1.6	1655	30.5	13.6	1630	12.0	12.0
OC13	79C	7.6	1654	9.6	21.6	0600	13.5	12.0
SW14	79C	9.6	1715	10.6	21.6	1400	11.9	11.3
34a	78BLBS	8.6	1610	9.6	20.6	1630	12.0	11.4
OC62	79GB	(2.7)–5.7[3]	1700	5.7	17.7	0600	11.5	11.5
							MEAN = 12.4	MEAN = 11.6

Notes
[1] Full incubation assumed from laying of third Reed Warbler egg at 0600 hours
[2] This egg assumed not laid earlier than noon: it was probably laid some hours later
[3] Egg removed from nest when laid on 2.7 and returned three days later at 1700 hours

it began at about 0600 hours on the laying day of the third egg) took on average 11.6 days.

The eggs of non-parasitic North American cuckoos hatch after an incubation period of only 10–11 days, even shorter than parasitic cuckoos, and possibly the shortest incubation period known in birds irrespective of size, weight or family. Presumably this rapid hatching time minimizes predation at the nest, and allows the fast-developing young to leave the nest soon for safety in the bushes. The advantage to parasitic cuckoos in having short incubation periods, however, is that they will hatch out in advance of their host's eggs, giving the young parasites a head start over their competitors in the nest. The young of several parasitic cuckoos now possess a further adaptation to promote their success, as we shall see in the next chapter.

Fates of Cuckoo eggs

There are few data available on the outcome of series of eggs laid by Cuckoos because most workers collected all the eggs that they found. As we have seen there are many reasons why Cuckoo eggs fail. An egg may miss the nest when laid, or be laid at the wrong time so that the hosts bury it in the nest-lining, or the young of the host hatch out sooner than the young Cuckoo. The egg may break when dropped into a nest, or the hosts may desert it or throw it out. It may be robbed by predators or destroyed by bad weather. Of 176 Cuckoo eggs I have found in Reed Warbler nests and 2 in Sedge Warbler nests in Cambridgeshire during six years, 5 were definitely deserted, 2 were buried in the nest-lining because they were laid before the warblers started their own clutch, 4 were infertile, 49 (28 per cent) disappeared from the nest, usually with the entire host's clutch during the incubation period and were presumed mostly predated, some of them by Cuckoos, and a total of 114 (65 per cent) hatched. Two eggs were not followed up at one of the subsidiary sites surveyed in 1979. The success of Cuckoo eggs in Reed Warbler nests, therefore, was evidently quite high especially in comparison with the Reed Warbler's high nesting failure. It would be interesting to compare success rates with different host species in different areas, but at present detailed records are lacking.

10 | Young

When it hatches in the host's nest, usually before the host's eggs, the young Cuckoo looks like any other nidicolous bird: blind, naked and apparently helpless. Most young birds at this stage can only raise their heads to gape for food. For the first few hours of its life, this is all that the young Cuckoo does, although for the most part it will be brooded by the fosterparent. Soon it begins to fidget and shows that it is not at all helpless, but possesses an adaptation unrivalled in other brood parasites: it physically ejects the unhatched eggs or newly-hatched young of the host from the nest, so it occupies the nest alone and receives all the food. The young Cuckoo is now reared to the total detriment of the host's brood. In the African honeyguides (Indicatoridae) and parasitic Striped Cuckoo, *Tapera naevia*, of South America among the other brood parasitic birds, the young are also reared to the exclusion of any of the host's young, but in their case the young are equipped with special mandibular hooks in their first days of existence with which they kill their foster siblings. In some cuckoos, the cowbirds, widowbirds and Black-headed Duck, the hosts rear some of their own young along with one or more young of the parasite.

Ejection behaviour

Edward Jenner, the inventor of vaccination, was the first observer to describe accurately the ejection behaviour by a young Cuckoo in the nest of a Dunnock in 1788. At this time, Jenner's graphic account was viewed with almost total disbelief. It was known that the young Cuckoo was reared alone in the nest, but generally thought that the adult Cuckoo returned to remove the host's eggs or young so that its own offspring would receive all the food. Few people at that time believed that a young nidicolous bird only a few hours or a day old could support even its own weight, let alone contrive to carry eggs and young on its back up the side of a nest to heave them over the edge. Since then, of course, it has been witnessed, described, filmed and photographed many times. It is instinctive behaviour in young European Cuckoos, as well as in the young of other parasitic cuckoos belonging to the genera *Cuculus*, *Chrysococcyx* and *Cacomantis*. Ejection behaviour is absent in *Eudynamis*, *Scythrops* and *Clamator*, possibly because the eggs of their hosts are much larger and more difficult to lift. Its occurrence in other cuckoos is unknown because their breeding biology has not yet been studied.

This remarkable instinct to eject anything in the nest does not normally manifest itself until several hours after the young Cuckoo hatches. By this time, it has dried out, received a few meals and gained in strength for the task it now has to perform to ensure its survival. From about 8–36 hours after hatching the young Cuckoo wriggles about in the bottom of the nest until it manoeuvres one of the host's eggs against the side of the nest. Its back has a slight hollow between the scapulars which traps an egg against the nest-wall. The Cuckoo's head is held down, almost touching its belly. Then with its feet apart and with muscular thighs, the youngster slowly works the egg up the side of the nest holding its tiny wings backward to prevent the egg from rolling off. When it nears the nest rim the wings clasp the top as the legs push up from the side of the nest. Balancing the egg on its back to the top of the nest, the young Cuckoo quivers and jerks for a few seconds and hangs there feeling with its wings to make sure the egg has gone over. Then it drops back into the nest-cup. Maybe only a few minutes later it will repeat the procedure with the next egg, and so on until the nest is empty.

Ejection continues even when the fosterparent is brooding, and it seems incredible that the parent host will lift itself up from the clutch to allow the young Cuckoo to accomplish its gruesome task. The host simply watches as its precious eggs or young are thrown overboard one by one. Even when they hang just outside the nest, caught in the vegetation or material of the nest, the hosts make no effort to retrieve their young, so that they die where they hang – producing a macabre picture. The hosts only recognize their young if they are well and truly in the nest, and as the young Cuckoo is there showing all the right signs to stimulate their parental instincts, they show no interest in their own displaced offspring.

Occasionally young Cuckoos accidentally eject themselves during these efforts to empty the nest. This happened on two occasions out of 114 young Cuckoos which hatched during my study, but could have occurred more frequently and gone undetected. In this event, the young Cuckoo suffers the same fate as the host's young and dies neglected because it is not in the proper place. Even more occasionally two Cuckoos hatch in the same nest. Usually the first to hatch will eject the other because it will be unlikely that both eggs were laid on the same day. When two young Cuckoos occupy the same nest the strongest will usually succeed in evicting the other. Molnar (1944) reported one case of a Great Reed Warbler nest containing three newly-hatched Cuckoos: the first was ejected quite soon after hatching, while the remaining two tried to eject each other for four days until they eventually both fell out of the nest. Molnar also stated that ejection sometimes began when the young Cuckoo was only three hours old, but this depended upon its size and circumstances. I, too, noticed that larger Cuckoo eggs produced heavier chicks at hatching, which ejected the nest contents more quickly than smaller chicks. This became apparent only during attempts to photograph the activity at different nests. Nevertheless, no young Cuckoo failed to eject the nest contents because of its smaller size. By the fourth day, the instinct to eject subsides and, if by some chance any host eggs or young remain, they are usually smothered by the rapid-growing Cuckoo so that they die and are removed by the fosterparents.

Amazingly, however, there are a few records of young Cuckoos being reared along with the young of their host, but these are exceptional. Burton (1947) found a Robin's nest on 3 June in which there were five host eggs and one of a Cuckoo. Four of the Robin's eggs hatched on 4 June, the fifth was infertile, and the Cuckoo hatched on the following day. On 7 June the young Cuckoo was observed repeatedly attempting to eject the young Robins but was unsuccessful. By the following day it had lost the urge and settled down on top of its nestmates. The outcome of this nest was that the young Cuckoo left the nest after a normal nestling time of 20 days, but the young Robins did not die – they fledged on 27 June when 23 days old or about 10 days later than normal. The chance of this happening in niche- or hole-nesting host species, when the young Cuckoo cannot dispose of the host's young because of the confines of the nest site, is higher than in host species with open nests. In Russia, Malchevsky (1960) photographed a young Cuckoo with a brood of young Redstarts soon after they had emerged from their nest on 18 June. Another surprising case was related by Chance (1940) where a gardener had exposed a nest of a Dunnock containing two young Cuckoos, both of which apparently survived to fledging. And in France, Claudon (1955) also claimed to have found two young Cuckoos with three young Great Grey Shrikes, *Lanius excubitor*, which all survived. In this case the author supposed that the young Cuckoos had been unable to eject the host's eggs because of their greater weight.

These instances of young Cuckoos being reared with the host young are made even more remarkable when considering the growth rates of the two.

Growth rates of young Cuckoos

The growth rate or rate of weight increase in a young European Cuckoo is about the same as the weight increase of the whole brood of chicks of the average passerine host (Figure 10). The main difference is that the young Cuckoo remains in the nest for about three weeks whereas the host's young would normally fledge after 1½–2 weeks. Reed Warblers usually fledge when they are 11 days old, while young Cuckoos reared by this host do not leave until they reach about 19 days old.

On hatching, the young Cuckoo weighs about 3–4g (Table 31). By the time it is only four days old, after the ejection period, a young Cuckoo has already reached the weight of one of its fosterparents – about four times its hatching weight at around 16g. At a week old it weighs about 37g or ten times its hatching weight. There is evidently a very rapid increase in weight until the Cuckoo reaches 11 days old which, in the case of Reed Warblers, is when the host young would leave the nest. The Cuckoo becomes more active at this stage – turning round in the nest,

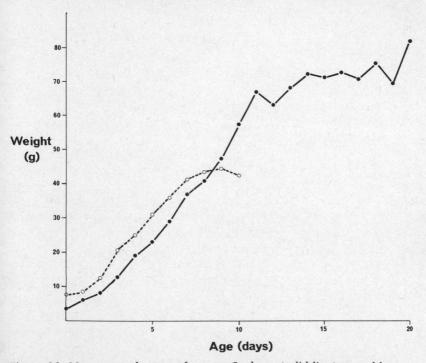

Figure 10. Mean growth rates of young Cuckoos (solid line) reared by Reed Warblers and broods of four young Reed Warblers (dashed line) in Cambridgeshire, 1975–1979

Table 31 *Growth rates (weights in grammes) of young European Cuckoos with different host species*

Age (days)	Cambridgeshire 1974–1979 (present study) Reed Warbler, *Acrocephalus scirpaceus*		Oxford 1946 (Werth 1947) Dunnock, *Prunella modularis*	Oxford 1947 (Werth 1947) Robin, *Erithacus rubecula*	Switzerland 1946 (in Werth 1947) White Wagtail *Motacilla alba*
	mean (range)	n			
0	3.6 (2.7–5.0)	13	3.6	–	3.0
1	6.1 (4.8–8.7)	8	5.4	–	–
2	8.1 (6.5–11.0)	9	7.5	8.0	–
3	12.8 (10.0–16.1)	7	11.4	11.6	12.8
4	19.1 (16–28)	9	16.4	16.4	18.5
5	23.1 (19–29)	9	21.2	21.6	23.0
6	28.9 (26–36)	6	26.8	31.0	31.0
7	37.0 (32–44)	7	32.9	37.5	42.0
8	40.8 (37–50)	7	41.1	45.5	–
9	47.4 (42–55)	10	47.7	54.0	60.0
10	57.5 (55–62)	4	54.5	62.0	–
11	67.0 (54–70)	11	60.0	69.0	72.0
12	63.3 (58–68)	3	71.0	72.0	–
13	68.3 (58–78)	6	78.5	78.5	86.0
14	72.2 (63–79)	4	81.0	81.0	–
15	71.2 (62–80)	6	83.5	89.0	94.0
16	72.7 (61–82)	6	86.5	95.5	98.0
17	70.8 (58–83)	7	87.0	100.0	97.0
18	75.4 (65–84)	5	83.0	99.5	100.0
19	69.5 (64–74)	4	85.0	106.5	98.0
20	82.0 (68–90)	3	85.0	–	–

wing-stretching, preening, etc. and its rate of growth slows down. Weights of young Cuckoos reared by four different host species (Table 31) show this decrease in growth rate from 11 days old, but those measured in Reed Warbler nests did not reach the higher weights of those raised by Dunnocks, Robins or White Wagtails recorded by Werth (1947). With the Dunnock a young Cuckoo increased in weight in 20 days from 3.6g to 85g; to 106.5g with the Robin; and from 3g to 98g with the White Wagtail in Switzerland. The maximum weight reached by a nestling Cuckoo reared by Reed Warblers in my study was 90g, but the average pre-fledging weight was 82g, somewhat lower than in the other three species in Table 31. It would obviously be interesting to compare growth rates of young Cuckoos raised by different species in more detail to see if some species are better than others.

Even when they become independent, young Cuckoos have relatively lower weights than adults, at least in Britain (Seel 1977a). By the time they reach southern Europe they are presumably much heavier, maybe adding as much as 50 per cent to their original independence weight before migrating into Africa.

When it first hatches a young Cuckoo is a uniform pink-flesh colour. It thus resembles some host young, but not others. Young Dunnocks, for example, are also flesh-coloured, whereas young Reed Warblers are blackish when they hatch. At one day old the young Cuckoo begins to darken, first on the head, then along the back, rump, wings, and later, underneath. By the time it is three days old, it has changed from a pink to an almost black colour, but is still naked and blind. From hatching the colour of the inside of the mouth is pale orange, the colour accentuating to deeper orange-red by the third day. The flanges of the gape are yellow at first, becoming orange a few days later. On the fourth day the feather quills emerge on the head, wings, tail and back, and the young Cuckoo fills the bottom of the nest. The eyes begin to open on the fifth day as more and more feather quills appear, and the youngster assumes a dark, prickly appearance. At this stage the fosterparents only brood the Cuckoo during spells of bad weather and at night; otherwise they are constantly bringing food to the seemingly insatiable youngster. On the seventh day the feathers begin to emerge and the eyes fully open. Now the young Cuckoo can see its foster-parents arriving with food, and its begging calls become more pronounced as it encourages them to bring food. Over the next few days the feathers emerge, so by the time it is nine days old the young Cuckoo has the appearance of a well-feathered youngster. In fact, of course, there are large areas of its body still bare. Only the head, chest and back (all the exposed areas) are well-feathered at this time because the hosts can no longer brood the youngster at night. Periods of excessive rain from now until the Cuckoo is ready to leave the nest can soak the unprotected youngster so that it dies of exposure. The hosts are already hopelessly outgrown and cannot protect it. In the case of Reed Warblers, with nests often exposed to wind and rain, many young Cuckoos come to grief for this reason. Another common cause of loss, particularly at my main study site situated along flood meadows of the River Ouse in Cambridgeshire, was flooding due to excessive rainfall in June or July.

Soon after the feathers emerge from their sheaths, the characteristic white occipital markings appear on the head, often in two spots – one on top of the head above the eyes, the other at the back. The young Cuckoo retains these markings throughout its juvenile plumage until its first moult in the winter. Some adults also have a few white tipped feathers on the head, but they are usually outnumbered and hidden by normal grey ones. In young Cuckoos, as discussed earlier, this may have a defensive purpose in mimicking young hawks. The tail feathers are also tipped white when they emerge, so the young Cuckoo has a speckled, rather alarming appearance which is augmented by its brilliant orange-red gape. Perhaps this strange appearance deters some potential enemies. The red mouth may act as a 'warning' sign to some potential predators. But it also serves as a stimulus to the hosts for the provision of food. The fact that other birds, beside the actual host pair, will feed a begging young Cuckoo suggests that it possesses some super-stimulus which passerines cannot ignore if they are in the food-bringing stage of their own breeding cycle. There is scope here for further experimentation: do the hosts preferentially feed a youngster with an orange gape rather than any other colour, or with large rather than small gape?

From 11 days old, when the rate of growth lessens, the young Cuckoo continues to grow its feathers which it now ruffles and preens when the hosts are away gathering food. At two weeks old it appears fully-feathered and completely fills the nest – projecting well over the top. Now it can be heard calling for food from some distance and is likely to attract predators by its incessant begging cries. From the time its eyes open at seven days old, it will lunge bravely at an approaching enemy, or even its fosterparent on occasions. The hosts remove encapsulated faeces which the young Cuckoo presents over the edge of the nest, but if attacked or handled, it produces a defensive, foul-smelling brown, liquid dropping. It also emits a hawk-like, rattling alarm call when handled from about 16 days old. By now the main flight feathers and tail have grown and the young Cuckoo spends much of its time preening and wing-stretching. Whenever the hosts come near it turns around in the nest to face them with its orange gape and insistent begging cries. When the hosts arrive with food it quivers one outstretched wing and vibrates its huge mouth. The nest may have been reduced to a flattened platform by now, and the young Cuckoo could easily lose its balance and fall out. On the ground it becomes easy prey for marauding mammalian predators, or it might drown in the water below.

From about 17 days old it is ready to leave the nest and can manage short, clumsy flights near the nest. During the next few days it scrambles about in a nearby bush or tree, demanding food from its fosterparents and any other birds which happen to come near. By the time it is 21 or 22 days old it can fly awkwardly, but well enough to keep out of danger from ground predators. It is now that it risks predation by hawks and owls. During the time it remains dependent upon the hosts for food, the young Cuckoo may travel several hundred metres from the nest-site, much further than the host's young would travel before fending for themselves. The host pair follow their young Cuckoo wherever it goes, providing it with food until it becomes independent. Because of its great size, the hosts sometimes have to stand on the Cuckoo's back to feed it. How long a young Cuckoo remains dependent on the hosts after fledging is difficult to determine with accuracy. In Reed Warblers, I have found that two or three weeks is the rule (Table 32), whereas other workers have suggested a 4–6 week post-fledging dependence period with different hosts.

Table 32 *Fledging and host-dependence periods of young Cuckoos reared by Reed Warblers in Cambridgeshire 1974–1979*

Nest No.	Date hatched	Date left nest	Age left nest (days)	Date able to fly	Age at first flight (days)	Date independent	Age at independence (days)
74.28	12.6	–	–	–	–	13.7	31
75.99	22.6	11.7	19	12.7	20	26.7	34
75.101	30.6	–	–	20.7	20	5.8	36
75.127	7.6	23.6	17	26.6	20	12.7	36
75.163	6.7	20.7	14	23.7	17	11.8	36
75.182	8.7	23.7	15	28.7	20	10.8	33
75.206	17.7	30.7	13	3.8	17	16.8	30
75.230	20.7	9.8	20	10.8	21	21.8	32
75.244	19.6	8.7	19	–	–	3.8	45
75.253	10.7	–	–	27.7	17	15.8	36
78.177	9.7	29.7	20	–	–	9.8	31
79.34a	20.6	–	–	9.7	19	18.7	28
79.OC19	24.6	–	–	–	–	23.7	29
79.251	18.7	–	–	–	–	13.8	26
		MEAN 17.1			19.0		33.1

Mortality

The mortality rate in young Cuckoos is evidently high. We have seen that there are many dangers: self-ejection, non-synchronized laying and inability to eject the host's young, flooding, waterlogging and exposure, nest-disintegration, desertion and predation. There are few figures for mortality rates in young Cuckoos because most finders of large enough numbers collected the eggs. Studying Cuckoos parasitizing mainly Dunnocks in Kent, Owen (1933) reported that, for various reasons, 73 (34 per cent) out of 213 young Cuckoos failed to fledge. In my study on Reed Warblers (one in a Sedge Warbler nest), a total of 114 young Cuckoos were known to hatch. The outcomes of 74 were known, Forty-eight (65 per cent) disappeared from the nest before they could fly, and were presumed predated. About half of these vanished when they were between one and two weeks old, with roughly equal numbers lost during the first and last weeks of the nestling period. Perhaps the noisier food-begging cries after a week attracted the attention of predators such as stoats, weasels, rats and crows. Two young Cuckoos accidentally fell out when ejecting the host's eggs or young, so they died below the nests. A further eight also died – one drowned when its nest became flooded, three drowned when they fell out of their nests into water, two were found dead below the nest, presumably deserted when the hosts found their nests empty, and two died in the nest, one at 11 days old from exposure to heavy rain, the other apparently through desertion or death of one fosterparent. (The single Reed Warbler in this case was unable to rear the young Cuckoo beyond 16 days when it lost weight and died.) Because time was limiting, I was unable to record the final outcome of 40 young Cuckoos, but nearly all of them were ringed or wing-tagged after reaching at least ten days old. Only 16 (22 per cent), out of the 74 young Cuckoos, were known to have reached independence.

In 1975–1978, I wing-tagged 38 young Cuckoos of which six died before reaching independence. Two were ringed only, and in 1979 a further 20 were ringed but not marked with wing-tags. In total, therefore, 60 nestling Cuckoos were marked during the study period. Only four of these returned in a subsequent year: one male returned in 1976, 1977 and 1978 to its natal area; another marked in 1977 came back in the next two years, and another marked in 1978 was seen again in the following year. A wing-tagged yearling female was seen on only two occasions early in its first season, but was never recorded again. Perhaps the tags came off, or the bird died or moved elsewhere to breed. These few returns were insufficient for my objectives. My technique of marking Cuckoos for individual recognition, therefore, proved unsuccessful in providing evidence for the inheritance of egg-colour and host-specificity. For this method to work, a much larger number of young Cuckoos would need to be marked, or catching techniques improved to trap most, if not all, of the birds using a breeding site during a number of years.

Despite the many drawbacks and difficulties, I still think that such a venture would be worthwhile. There is much scope for learning more about the biology and behaviour of the Cuckoo, and other brood parasitic birds, by studying a population of marked individuals. For such a project to be a success in the future, clearly a great deal more time and resources than I had at my disposal would be necessary. Essential to this study would be a suitable breeding site where it would be possible to catch the birds, where they could be seen regularly or followed by radio-telemetry, and where the nests of the hosts could be easily found. Such places are rapidly becoming more and more difficult to find in Europe — so good use should be made of them lest they all disappear.

Bibliography

Ackworth, B., 1955, *Bird and Butterfly Mysteries*, Eyre & Spottiswoode, London

Ali, S. A., 1931, 'The origin of mimicry in cuckoo eggs', *J. Bombay Nat. Hist. Soc.* **34**: 1067–1070

Ali, S. A., and Ripley, S. D., 1969, *Handbook of the birds of India and Pakistan*, Vol. 3. Bombay, Oxford Univ. Press

Anon, 1961, 'Strange Cuckoo behaviour', *Countryside* **19**: 203

Armitage, J. S., 1978, 'Feeding methods and prey of Cuckoo', *Brit. Birds* **71**: 590

Ash, J. S., 1965, 'The "raptor-flight" of the Cuckoo', *Brit. Birds* **58**: 1–5

Baird, D. A., 1945, 'A note on *Lampromorpha klaasi* (Stephens) and the care of its young', *Ibis* **87**: 565–566

Baker, E. C. Stuart, 1923, 'Cuckoos' eggs and evolution', *Proc. Zool. Soc. London* 1923: 277–294

Baker, E. C. Stuart, 1942, *Cuckoo Problems*, Witherby, London

Baldamus, E., 1868, 'Fresh contributions to the history of the propagation of the European Cuckoo (*Cuculus canorus*).' Translated in *Zoologist* Series 2. **3**: 1146–1166

Baldamus, E., 1892, *Das Leben der Europäischen Kuckucke, nebst Beiträgen zur Lebenskunde der übrigen parasitischen Kuckucke und Stärlinge.* Parey, Berlin

Bannerman, D. A., 1955, *The Birds of the British Isles Vol. IV*, Oliver and Boyd, London

Beal, F. E. L., 1898, 'The food of cuckoos'. In Beal, F. E. L. & Judd, S. D. (eds), 'Cuckoos and shrikes in their relation to agriculture', *Bull. U.S. Dept. Agric.* **9**: 7–14

Bell, A. P., 1965, 'Observer mobbed by adult Cuckoo when approaching juvenile', *Brit. Birds* **58**: 150

Benson, G. B. G., 1959, 'Adult male Cuckoo being fed by Dunnock', *Brit. Birds* **52**: 269

Bent, A. C., 1940, 'Life histories of North American cuckoos, goatsuckers, hummingbirds and their allies', *U.S. Nat. Mus. Bull.* **176**

Beven, G., 1943, 'Some notes from Oudtshoorn', *Ostrich* 13: 235–238

Blaise, M., 1965, 'Contribution a l'étude de la reproduction du Coucou gris *Cuculus canorus* dans la nord-est de la France', *L'Oiseau et R.F.O.* 35: 87–116

Bottomley, J. B., and Bottomley, S., 1975, 'Cuckoos photographed feeding on Magpie Moth caterpillars', *Brit. Birds* 68: 514

Brown, P. E., and Davies, M. G., 1949, *Reed-Warblers*, Foy Publications Ltd, East Molesey

Brühn, P., 1960, 'Beitrag zur pflege des Kuckucks', *Gefied. Welt.* 84: 173

Bruns, H., and Nocke, H., 1959, 'Die Erstankunit des Kuckucks (*Cuculus canorus*) in Deutschland 1948–1957', *Orn. Mitt.* Stuttgart 11: 70–78

Buchan-Hepburn, J., 1955, 'Cuckoo in Surrey in February', *Brit. Birds* 48: 512

Burton, J. G., 1900, 'Curious note of a Cuckoo', *Irish Nat.* 9: 186

Burton, R. E., 1947, 'Robins rearing own young and Cuckoo in same nest', *Brit. Birds* 40: 149–150

Capek, V., 1896, 'Beiträge zur Fortpflanzungsgeschichte des Kuckucks', *Orn. Jahrb.* 7: 41–72, 102–117, 146–157, 165–183

Chalk, A. S., 1950, 'Strange behaviour of a cuckoo', *Emu* 49: 219–220

Chance, E., 1922, *The Cuckoo's Secret*, Sidgwick & Jackson, London

Chance, E., 1940, *The Truth about the Cuckoo*, Country Life, London

de Chavigny, J. 1934, 'Autour du coucou (*Cuculus canorus canorus*)', *Alauda* 6: 502–511

Claudon, A., 1955, 'Nouvelles observations sur *Cuculus c. canorus* Linné en Alsac', *L'Oiseau et R.F.O.* 25: 44–49

Claudon, A., 1956, 'Le Coucou gris *Cuculus canorus canorus*, Linné en Alsace', *Bull. Soc. Hist. nat. Colmar* 46: 41–62.

Clay, T. and Meinertzhagen, R., 1933, 'La vie avienne des Hautes-Pyrenees', *Oiseau (N.S.)* 3: 563–580

Collinge, W. E., 1925, *The food of some British wild birds*, Part 5. Yorkshire Herald Newspaper Company Ltd, York

de la Comble, J., 1958, 'Dates de pontes remarquables du coucou (*Cuculus canorus*) dans l'Autunois', *Alauda* 26: 152

Condry, W. M., 1966, *The Snowdonia National Park*, Collins, London

Cooper, R. P., 1958, 'Pallid Cuckoo feeding young', *Emu* 58: 67–68

Courtney, J. 1967, 'The juvenile food-begging call of some fledgling cuckoos – vocal mimicry or vocal duplication by natural selection?', *Emu* 67: 154–157

Crawshaw, K. R., 1963, 'Juvenile Cuckoo's method of feeding upon Cinnabar Moth caterpillars', *Brit. Birds* 56: 28

Cronin, E. W., and Sherman, P. W., 1977, 'A resource-based mating system: the Orange-rumped Honeyguide *Indicator xanthonotus*', *Living Bird* **15**: 5–32

Curtis, B., 1969, 'Observations on Wren rearing young Cuckoo', *Brit. Birds* **62**: 117–119

Darwin, C., 1872, *The Origin of Species*, The New American Library (6th Edition), New York

Davis, D. E., 1942, 'The phylogeny of social nesting habits in the Crotophaginae', *Quart. Rev. Biol.* **17**: 115–134

Dement'ev, G. P., and Gladkov, N. A., (eds) 1966, *Birds of the Soviet Union*, *Vol. 1.* (translated from Russian by Birron, A. and Cole, Z. S.), Israel Program for Scientific Translations, Jerusalem

De Smet, W. M. A., 1967, 'Studie over de trek van de Koekoek *Cuculus canonus* L. Eerste Deel: Beschouwingen over de waarde van de aankomstdata, *Gerfaut* **57**: 50–76

De Smet, W. M. A., 1970, 'Studie over de trek van de Koekoek *Cuculus canorus* L. Tweede deel: De Lentetrek van de Koekoek doorheen Europa. Ontleding van eigen gegevans', *Gerfaut* **60**: 148–187

Dooly, T. L. S., 1928, 'Cuckoos returning to same summer quarters for nine and ten successive years', *Brit. Birds* **22**: 23–24

Edwards, G., Hosking, E., and Smith, S., 1949, 'Reactions of some passerine birds to a stuffed Cuckoo', *Brit. Birds* **42**: 13–19

Edwards, G., Hosking, E., and Smith, S., 1950, 'Reactions of some passerine birds to a stuffed Cuckoo II. A detailed study of the willow-warbler', *Brit. Birds* **43**: 144–150

Evans, G. H., 1969, 'Birds singing in lighthouse beams', *Brit. Birds* **63**: 79

Field, J., 1962, 'Bird Report for 1961', *Middle-Thames Naturalist*, **No. 14**: 1961: 21

Fraga, R. M., 1978, 'The rufous-collared sparrow as a host of the shiny cowbird', *Wilson Bull.* **90**: 271–284

Friedmann, H. 1929, *The Cowbirds: A Study in the Biology of Social Parasitism*, Thomas, Springfield, Ill.

Friedmann, H., 1948, 'The parasitic cuckoos of Africa', *Wash. Acad. Sci. Monogr.* 1

Friedmann, H., 1949, 'Additional data on African parasitic cuckoos', *Ibis* **91**: 514–519

Friedmann, H., 1956, 'Further data on African parasitic cuckoos', *Proc. U.S. Nat. Mus.* **106**: 377–408

Friedmann, H., 1964, 'Evolutionary trends in the avian genus *Clamator*', *Smithson. Misc. Collect.* **146**: 1–127

Friedmann, H., 1967, 'Alloxenia in three sympatric African species of *Cuculus*', *Proc. U.S. Nat. Mus. Bull.* **124**: 1–14

Friedmann, H., 1968, 'The evolutionary history of the avian genus *Chrysoccoccyx*', *U.S. Nat. Mus. Bull.* **265**

Gaston, A. J., 1976, 'Brood parasitism by the Pied Crested Cuckoo, *Clamator jacobinus*', *J. Anim. Ecol.* **45**: 331–348

Gautier, F., 1968, 'Deux jeunes coucous nourris par un couple de rougequeues noirs', *Nos Oiseaux* **29**: 235

Gervis, G. R., 1966, '"Raptor-flight" of Cuckoo', *Brit. Birds*, **59**: 434

Glue, D., and Morgan, R., 1972, 'Cuckoo hosts in British habitats', *Bird Study*, **19**: 187–192

Godfrey, R., 1939, 'The black-crested cuckoo', *Ostrich*, **10**: 21–27

Green, C. E., 1928, 'The Cuckoo', *J. Northants Nat. Hist. Soc. Fld. Cl.* **25** (194): 145–147

Gurney, J. H., 1899, 'The Economy of the Cuckoo (*Cuculus canorus*)', *Trans. Norfolk and Norwich Nat. Soc.* **6**: 365–384

Hamilton, W. J., and Hamilton, M. E., 1965, 'Breeding characteristics of yellow-billed cuckoos in Arizona', *Proc. Calif. Acad. Sci., 4th Ser.*, **32**: 405–432

Hamilton, W. J., and Orians, G. H., 1965, 'Evolution of brood parasitism in altricial birds', *Condor*, **67**: 361–382

Hardy, J., 1879, 'Popular history of the Cuckoo', *Folk Lore Record*, Vol. 2: 47–91, Folk Lore Soc

Harrison, C. J. O., 1975, *A field guide to the nests, eggs and nestlings of British and European Birds*, Collins, London

Haydock, E. L., 1950, 'Supplementary notes on African cuckoos', *Ibis* **92**: 149–150

Headley, F. W. and Jourdain, F. C. R., 1919, 'Adult Cuckoo killing nestling birds', *Brit. Birds* **13**: 57

Hereford Ornithological Club, 1954, Annual Report, *Brit. Birds*, **47**: 212

Herrick, F. H., 1910, 'Life and behavior of the cuckoo', *J. Exp. Zool.* **9**: 169–233

Hickman, C. F., 1975, 'Cuckoo calls', *Field*, **246** (6373): 482

Holliday, C. S. and Tait, I. C., 1953, 'Notes on the nidification of *Buccanodon olivacea woodwardi* (Shelley)', *Ostrich* **24**: 115–117

Howe, F. E., 1905, 'Field notes on cuckoos', *Emu* **5**: 35–36

Humphreys, G. R., 1924, 'Observations on a female Cuckoo', *Irish Nat.* **33**: 118–121

Hunter, H. C., 1961, 'Parasitism of the masked weaver *Ploceus velatus arundinaceus*', *Ostrich* **32**: 55–63

Hursthouse, E. W., 1944, In 'Summarized notes', *New Zealand Bird Notes*, **1**: 78

Ishizawa, J., and Chiba, S., 1966, 'Food analysis of four species of cuckoos in Japan', *Misc. Rep. Yamashima Inst. Orn.* **4**: 302–326

Jackson, F. J., 1938, *The birds of Kenya Colony and the Uganda Protectorate*, London

Jenner, E., 1788, 'Observations on the natural history of the Cuckoo', *Phil. Trans. Roy. Soc. London.* **78**: 219–235

Jensen, R. A. C., and Clinning, C. F., 1975, 'Breeding biology of two cuckoos and their hosts in South West Africa', *Living Bird* **13**: 5–50

Jensen, R. A. C., and Vernon, C. J., 1970, 'On the biology of the Didric Cuckoo in southern Africa', *Ostrich* **41**: 237–246

Jones, J. M., 1967, '"Raptor-flight" of Cuckoos', *Brit. Birds* **60**: 370

Jourdain, F. C. R., 1924, 'Early laying of Cuckoo', *Brit. Birds* **18**: 78–79

Jourdain, F. C. R., 1925, 'A study on parasitism in the cuckoos', *Proc. Zool. Soc. London* 1925: 639–667

Joy, N. H., 1943, 'How a Cuckoo laid into a Reed-Warbler's nest', *Brit. Birds* **36**: 176–8

King, B., 1937, 'Young Cuckoo in November in Sussex', *Brit. Birds* **31**: 236

Klaas, E. E., 1975, 'Cowbird parasitism and nesting success in the eastern phoebe', *Occas. Pap. Mus. Nat. Hist. Univ. Kans.* **41**: 1–18

Labitte, A., 1957, 'Observations sur le coucou', *L'Oiseau et R.F.O.* **28**: 153–162

Lack, D., 1956, *Swifts in a Tower*, Methuen, London

Lack, D., 1963, 'Cuckoo hosts in England', *Bird Study* **10**: 185–203

Lack, D., 1968, *Ecological Adaptations for Breeding in Birds*, Methuen, London

Lamba, B. S., 1963, 'The nidification of some common Indian birds', *J. Bombay Nat. Hist. Soc.* **60**: 121–133

Lancum, F. H., 1925, 'Early laying of Cuckoo in Essex', *Brit. Birds* **18**: 56–57

Latter, H. O., 1902, 'The egg of Cuculus canorus', *Biometrika* **1**: 164–176

Latter, H. O., 1905, 'The egg of Cuculus canorus', *Biometrika* **4**: 363–373

Liversidge, R., 1961, 'Pre-incubation development of *Clamator jacobinus*', *Ibis* **103a**: 624

Liversidge, R., 1971, 'The biology of the Jacobin Cuckoo *Clamator jacobinus*', *Proc. 3rd Pan-Afr. Ornithol. Congr., Ostrich Suppl.* **8**: 117–137

Löhrl, H., 1979, 'Untersuchungen am Kuckuck, *Cuculus canorus* (Biologie, Ethologie und Morphologie)', *J. Orn.* **120**: 139–173

Lowe, P. R., 1943, 'Some notes on the anatomical differences between the Cuculidae and the Musophagidae, with special reference to the specialization of the oesophagus in *Cuculus canorus* Linnaeus', *Ibis* **85**: 490–515

Maclaren, P. I. R., 1952, 'Feeding by the Didric Cuckoo', *Ibis* **94**: 684–685

Malchevsky, A. S., 1960, 'On the biological races of the Common Cuckoo *Cuculus canorus* L. in the territory of the European part of the USSR', *XII Int. Ornithol. Congr.*, *Helsinki*, 1958: 464–470

Marchant, S., 1972, 'Destruction of nest contents by cuckoos', *Emu* **72**: 29–31

Meinertzhagen, R., 1948, 'The birds of Ushant, Brittany', *Ibis* **90**: 553–567

Meinertzhagen, R., 1955, 'Speed and altitude of bird flight', *Ibis* **97**: 95

Meinertzhagen, R., 1959, *Pirates and Predators: The piratical and predatory habits of birds*, Oliver & Boyd, Edinburgh and London

Menzel, H., 1970, 'Zur Eiblage des Kuckucks (*Cuculus canorus*)', *Vogelwelt* **91**: 154

Milburn, C. E., 1915, 'Adult Cuckoo killing nestling Meadow Pipits', *Brit. Birds* **9**: 95–96

Millar, H. M., 1943, 'The Emerald Cuckoo', *Ostrich* **14**: 118

Molnar, B., 1944, 'The Cuckoo in the Hungarian plain', *Aquila* (Budapest) **51**: 100–112

Moreau, R. E., 1944, 'Food-bringing by African Bronze cuckoos', *Ibis*, **86**: 98–100

Moreau, R. E., 1966, *The Bird Faunas of Africa and its Islands*, Academic Press, New York and London

Moreau, R. E., 1972, *The Palaearctic-African Bird Migration Systems* Academic Press, New York and London

Moreau, R. E., and Moreau, W. M., 1939, 'Observations on some East African birds', *Ibis* **3**: 296–323

Morel, M. Y., 1973, 'Contribution à l'étude dynamique de la population de *Lagonosticta senegala* L (estrildides) à Richard-Toll (Sénégal). Interrelations avec le parasite *Hypochera chalybeata* (Müller) (viduines)', *Mem. Mus. Nat. d'Hist. Nat. Ser. A Zool.* **78**: 1–156

Mountfort, G., 1958, *Portrait of a wilderness. The story of the Coto Donãna Expeditions*, Hutchinson, London

Mundy, P. J., 1973, 'Vocal mimicry of their hosts by nestlings of the Great Spotted Cuckoo and Striped Crested Cuckoo', *Ibis*, **115**: 602–604

Mundy, P. J., and Cook, A. W., 1977, 'Observations on the breeding of the Pied Crow amd Great Spotted Cuckoo in northern Nigeria', *Ostrich* **48**: 72–84

Nicolai, J., 1974, 'Mimicry in parasitic birds', *Scient. Amer.* **231**: 93–98

Nisbet, I. C. T., 1957, 'Scandinavian passerine migration', *Ibis* **99**: 268

Nolan, V., and Thompson, C. F., 1975, 'The occurrence and significance of anomalous reproductive activities in two North American non-parasitic cuckoos', *Ibis*, **117**: 496–503

Ohmart, R. D., 1973, 'Observations on the breeding adaptations of the Roadrunner', *Condor* **75**: 140–149

Osmaston, B. B., 1916, 'Notes on cuckoos at Maymyo', *J. Bombay Nat. Hist. Soc.* **24**: 359–363

Owen, J. H., 1912, 'Wrens as foster-parents of the Cuckoo', *Brit. Birds* **6**: 91–92

Owen, J. H., 1933, 'The Cuckoo in the Felsted district', *Rep. Felsted School Sci. Soc.* **33**: 25–39

Palmer, M. G., 1946, *The Fauna and Flora of the Ilfracombe District of North Devon*, Townsend, Exeter

Parslow, J., 1973, *Breeding Birds of Britain and Ireland*, Berkhampstead

Paulussen, W., 1957, 'Nieuwe gegevens over de eieren, de waarden en de biologie van de Koekoek, *Cuculus canorus* L', *Gerfaut* **47**: 241–258

Payn, W. A., 1938, 'Spring migration at Tangier', *Ibis (Series 14)*, **2**: 33, 37

Payne, R. B., 1967, 'Interspecific communication signals in parasitic birds', *Am. Nat.* **101**: 363–375

Payne, R. B., 1973, 'Individual laying histories and the clutch size and numbers of eggs of parasitic cuckoos', *Condor*, **75**: 414–438

Payne, R. B., 1974, 'The evolution of clutch size and reproductive rates in parasitic cuckoos', *Evolution* **28**: 169–181

Payne, R. B., 1977, 'The ecology of brood parasitism in birds', *Ann. Rev. Ecol. Syst.* **8**: 1–28

Payne, R. B., and Payne, K., 1967, 'Cuckoo hosts in southern Africa', *Ostrich* **38**: 135–143

Pemberton, J. R., 1925, 'Parasitism in the Roadrunner', *Condor* **27**: 35

Perrins, C. M., 1967, 'The short apparent incubation period in the Cuckoo', *Brit. Birds* **60**: 51–52

Pounds, H. E., 1965, 'The "raptor-flight" of the Cuckoo', *Brit. Birds* **58**: 154–155

Radford, A. P., 1965, 'The "raptor-flight" of the Cuckoo', *Brit. Birds* **58**: 155

Ralph, C. P., 1975, 'Life style of *Coccyzus pumilus*, a tropical cuckoo', *Condor* **77**: 60–72

Rand, A. L., 1936, 'The Habits and distribution of Madagascar birds', *Bull. Amer. Mus. Nat. Hist.* **72**: 143–499

Rappe, A., 1965, 'Notes sur le passage diurne de la Tourerelle des Bois *Streptopelia turtur* et du Coucou *Cuculus canorus*', *Aves* **2**: 27–31

Reed, R. A., 1968, 'Studies of the Diederik Cuckoo *Chrysococcyx caprius* in the Transvaal', *Ibis* **110**: 321–331

Rensch, B., 1924, 'Zur Entstehung der Mimikry der Kuckuckseier', *J. Ornithol.* **72**: 461–472

Rey, E., 1892, *Altes und Neues aus dem Haushalte des Kuckucks*, Freese, Leipzig

Rey, E., 1894, 'Beobachtungen über den Kuckuck bei Leipzig aus dem Jahre 1893', *Ornithol. Monatschrift Dtsch. Vereins Schutze Vogelwelt* **19**: 159–168

Robertson, R. J., and Norman, R. F., 1976, 'Behavioral defenses to brood parasitism by potential hosts of the brown-headed cowbird', *Condor* **78**: 166–173

Roch, J., and Roberts, J. D. H., 1955, 'Cuckoo in Pembrokeshire in December', *Brit. Birds* **48**, 512

Royama, T., 1963, 'Appendix. Cuckoo hosts in Japan', *Bird Study*, **10**: 201–202

Royama, T., 1966, 'A re-interpretation of courtship feeding', *Bird Study* **13**: 116–129

Ruttledge, R. F., 1921, 'Ornithological notes from Mayo and Galway', *Irish Nat.* **30**: 46–49

Salvan, J., 1967–1969, 'Contribution a l'étude des oiseaux du Tchad', *Oiseau Revue fr. Orn.* **37**: 255–284; **38**: 53–85, 127–150, 249–273; **39**: 38–69

Scholey, G. J., 1927, 'Abnormal laying of Cuckoo', *Brit. Birds* **21**: 179

Seel, D. C., 1973, 'Egg-laying by the Cuckoo', *Brit. Birds* **66**: 528–534

Seel, D. C., 1977a, 'Trapping season and body size in the Cuckoo'. *Bird Study* **24**: 114–118

Seel, D. C., 1977b, 'Migration of the northwestern European population of the Cuckoo *Cuculus canorus*, as shown by ringing', *Ibis* **119**: 309–322

Serventy, D. L., and Whittell, H. M., 1962, *Birds of Western Australia*, Paterson Brokensha Pty. Ltd, Perth

Sharrock, J. T. R., 1973, *The Natural History of Cape Clear Island*, Berkhamstead

Sharrock, J. T. R., 1976, ed., *The Atlas of Breeding Birds in Britain and Ireland*, British Trust for Ornithology

Skutch, A. F., 1959, 'Life-history of the Groove-billed Ani', *Auk* **76**: 281–317

Skutch, A. F., 1966, 'Life history notes on three tropical American cuckoos', *Wilson Bull.* **78**: 139–165

Smith, K. D., 1957, 'An annotated check list of the birds of Eritrea, Part 2', *Ibis* **99**: 307–337

Smith, K. D., 1968, 'Spring migration through southeast Morocco', *Ibis* **110**: 452–492

Smith, N. G., 1968, 'The advantage of being parasitized', *Nature* **219**: 690–694

Smith, S. and Hosking, E., 1955, *Birds Fighting. Experimental studies of the aggressive displays of some birds*, Faber & Faber, London

Sokolowski, I., 1958, *Ptaki ziem Polskich*, Warsaw

Southern, H. N., 1954, 'Mimicry in cuckoos' eggs', in *Evolution as a Process*, ed. J. Huxley, A. C. Hardy, E. B. Ford. Allen & Unwin, London

Spector, W. S., 1956, ed. *Handbook of Biological Data*

Spencer, O. R., 1943, 'Nesting habits of the Black-billed Cuckoo', *Wilson Bull.* **55**: 11–22

Stresemann, E., and Stresemann, V., 1961, 'Die Handschwingen-Mauser der Kuckuck (Cuculidae)', *J. Orn.* **102**: 317–352

Swynnerton, C. F. M., 1918, 'Rejection by birds of eggs unlike their own; with remarks on some of the cuckoo problems', *Ibis* 1918: 27–54

Thomas, B. T., 1978, 'The dwarf cuckoo in Venezuela', *Condor* **80**: 105–106

Townley, D., 1936, 'Field notes on little known Southern Rhodesian birds', *Ostrich* **7**: 103–108

Uttendörfer, O., 1952, Neue Ergebnisse über die Ernährung der Greifvögel und Euler, Eugen Ubner, Stuttgart

Van De Weyer, B., 1928, 'Cuckoo returning to same summer quarters for nine and ten successive years', *Brit. Birds* **22**: 23–24

Valverde, J. A., 'Notas sobre la biologia de reproduction del Crialo *Clamator glandarius* (L)', *Ardeola* (numero especial): 591–647

Vehrencamp, S. L., 1976, 'The evolution of communal nesting in groove-billed anis', Ph.D. diss., Cornell Univ.

Vernon, C. J., 1971, 'Notes on the biology of the Black Coucal', *Ostrich* **42**: 242–258

Verheyen, R., 1950, 'La mue du coucou d'Europe. *Cuculus c. canorus* L', *Gerfaut* **40**: 212–231

Verheyen, R., 1951, 'Particularités relatives a la migration et au quartier d'hiver du coucou d'Europe (*Cuculus canorus* L.)', *Gerfaut* **41**: 44–61

Victoria, J. K., 1972, 'Clutch characteristics and egg discriminative ability of the African Village Weaverbird *Ploceus cucullatus*', *Ibis* **114**: 367–376

Voipio, P., 1953, 'The hepaticus variety and the juvenile types of the Cuckoo', *Ornis Fenn.* **30**: 97–117

Walter, A., 1889, 'Zur Fraga: Brütet der Kuckuck?' *Zoologist* 1889: 219–225

Ward, P., 1979, *Colour for Survival*, Orbis, London

Weller, M. W., 1968, 'The breeding biology of the parasitic black-headed duck', *Living Bird* **7**: 169–207

Werth, I., 1947, 'The growth of a young Cuckoo', *Brit. Birds* **40**: 331–334

Whitear, W., 1884, 'Early Cuckoo arrivals', *Trans. Norfolk and Norwich Nat. Soc.* **3**: 235–262

Whitson, M., 1976, 'Courtship behavior of the greater roadrunner', *Living Bird* **14**: 215–255

Wilde, N. A. J., 1974, 'Observations on Wren rearing young Cuckoo', *Brit. Birds* **67**: 26–27

Winterbottom, J. M., 1939, 'Miscellaneous notes on some birds of Northern Rhodesia', *Ibis* (Series 14) **3**: 712–734

Witherby, H. F., Jourdain, F. C. R., Ticehurst, N. F., and Tucker, B. W., 1938–1941, *The Handbook of British Birds*, Witherby, London

Worman, A. G., 1930, 'Male emerald cuckoo (*Chrysococcyx cupreus intermedius*) feeding young', *Ool. Rec.* **10**: 76–77

Wright, R. C. H., 1955, 'Cuckoo eating whole clutch of Dunnock's eggs', *Brit. Birds* **48**: 456–457

Wyllie, I., 1975, 'Study of Cuckoos and Reed Warblers', *Brit. Birds* **68**: 369–378

Yapp, W. B., 1962, *Birds and Woods*, Oxford University Press

Index